A Family Business Publication

Family Business Publications are the combined efforts of the Family Business Consulting Group and Palgrave Macmillan. These books provide useful information on a broad range of topics that concern the family business enterprise, including succession planning, communication, strategy and growth, family leadership, and more. The books are written by experts with combined experiences of over a century in the field of family enterprise and who have consulted with thousands of enterprising families the world over, giving the reader practical, effective, and time-tested insights to everyone involved in a family business.

More information about this series at
http://www.springer.com/series/14368

Stephanie Brun de Pontet

Transitioning from the Top

Personal Continuity Planning for the Retiring Family Business Leader

palgrave
macmillan

Stephanie Brun de Pontet
The Family Business Consulting Group, Inc.,
Chicago, Illinois, United States

A Family Business Publication
ISBN 978-1-349-95421-6   ISBN 978-1-137-57804-4 (eBook)
DOI 10.1057/978-1-137-57804-4

© The Editor(s) (if applicable) and The Author(s) 2018
Softcover reprint of the hardcover 1st edition 2017
This work is subject to copyright. All rights are solely and exclusively licensed by the Publisher, whether the whole or part of the material is concerned, specifically the rights of translation, reprinting, reuse of illustrations, recitation, broadcasting, reproduction on microfilms or in any other physical way, and transmission or information storage and retrieval, electronic adaptation, computer software, or by similar or dissimilar methodology now known or hereafter developed.
The use of general descriptive names, registered names, trademarks, service marks, etc. in this publication does not imply, even in the absence of a specific statement, that such names are exempt from the relevant protective laws and regulations and therefore free for general use.
The publisher, the authors and the editors are safe to assume that the advice and information in this book are believed to be true and accurate at the date of publication. Neither the publisher nor the authors or the editors give a warranty, express or implied, with respect to the material contained herein or for any errors or omissions that may have been made. The publisher remains neutral with regard to jurisdictional claims in published maps and institutional affiliations.

Cover image © Ashley Gerou / Shutterstock

Printed on acid-free paper

This Palgrave Macmillan imprint is published by Springer Nature
The registered company is Nature America Inc.
The registered company address is: 1 New York Plaza, New York, NY 10004, U.S.A.

Preface

Philippe Baillargeon never got to see the full fruits of his labors. A driven and determined man, he built a family business in road construction that a few years ago celebrated its 75th year in operation, and is in the 4th generation of family leadership. But he died in his 50s of a heart attack. I know this because Philippe was my maternal grandfather.

Contrast his story to that of my paternal grandfather: Dr. Andre Brun de Pontet. Also very driven, his sense of curiosity and the circumstances of WWII meant he pursued a variety of professional roles including those of international attorney and founder of a small Wall Street brokerage business. Throughout his working life and well beyond it, he was an avid traveler with an inquisitive mind, involved in everything from building collections for Paris's *Musée de l'Homme* to taking an active role with the Knights of Malta in France. 'Dadika' lived well into his 90s, chasing solar eclipses, promoting appreciation of art and culture, and pursuing other adventures that moved his mind and spirit.

Growing up in a family with two successful, charismatic grandfathers who are central to my family's narrative, I have always been drawn to "larger than life" personas, those people who, to quote Steve Jobs, "put a dent in the universe." Whether their field is business, research, sports, or entertainment, these are the distinctive individuals who are able to focus more, work harder, or come up with the paradigm-shifting innovations that set their accomplishments apart from others.

But what happens after the professional part of their lives – after the curtain closes on the careers they've held for decades, and how ready are they for that next life stage? Seeing my grandfathers' very different trajectories – one never made it to his twilight years and one had a long and fulfilling post-work life – made me think about the idea of "personal continuity" long before I called it that. I never met my grandfather Philippe (he died well before I was born), but growing up, I was very close to Dadika. As a result, even as a teenager I had an appreciation for the energy, ideas, and capacity of our society's "senior generation" – something our youth-obsessed culture tends to overlook and undervalue – and how those happiest in their senior years have often laid the groundwork for a satisfying late-life stage long before.

I have carried those interests and insights into my many years of work with family businesses. As a consultant I have had the great fortune to meet numerous successful business leaders, whose extraordinary careers have had a powerful impact on their companies, families, and communities. Not surprisingly, these individuals are often passionate about their business, put their heart and soul into their work, and derive a great deal of satisfaction from the impact they achieve through their careers and other activities.

While I admire deeply the contributions these individuals make to society – by solving business and social problems, creating employment opportunities, funding meaningful causes, and others – I also understand that this sort of success cannot happen without significant effort, risk, and sacrifice. A sacrifice that is often borne not only by that individual, but also the larger *system* in which they exist, especially their families. Sometimes the cost is steep but well-understood and willingly shared by the system; sometimes it is deferred or poorly understood, or shouldered primarily by one person.

In my advising work I have seen many situations where family enterprise leaders sacrifice their health or relationships to move their business toward ever-greater success. While this can create frustration and pain, for some these are intentional choices, sacrifices made with open eyes and a willingness to accept any trade-offs. An analogy would be the choices made by a young athlete with great potential; if they wish to succeed at the Olympics or on some other global stage, they (and their family) will have to forgo many aspects of a "normal" childhood and young adulthood for long hours of training and preparation, and may do so willingly.

The ultimate effects of that sacrifice vary. Some individuals are so focused on their long-term objectives that they may not be aware of the costs this single-minded journey incurs in other facets of their life. Their path is so linear that they have nowhere to go and no sources of fulfillment when they reach the end of that road. I have seen multiple successful CEOs shocked to realize how impoverished their personal relationships have become by the end of their professional tenure, and deeply frustrated by their inability to find meaningful pursuits and challenges outside of their business role. The resulting sense of emptiness can be profound; what's more, the fear of confronting this reality often plays a significant role in the leadership transition challenges so common in family-owned enterprises. The irony, of course, is that a failure to address the issue of personal continuity puts the continuity of the family business (for which that CEO has sacrificed so much) at serious risk, along with creating negative outcomes for the broader system, including family relationships and other components.

On the other hand, I have also met many family business leaders who have found the right balance: They have made significant sacrifices, worked hard, and invested consistently in the growth of their enterprise *while* developing and maintaining other outside personal interests. When these leaders transition away from the CEO role, they have other well-developed passions to pursue. That enables them to feel relevant and energized in spheres outside their role with the family business, and makes the loss of that central role less painful for them, and less burdensome for the system around them. In short, such individuals have explored and invested in the "side roads" on their journey, giving them access to more – and more fulfilling – options at the conclusion of their formal careers and making their transition easier for the entire family, including as this relates to the business succession.

That brings us to the motivation for this book.

Having observed a wide range of issues related to personal continuity over many years of client work, I wanted to explore this topic in greater depth, to better understand the journeys of CEOs who have found purpose and joy in their post-CEO vocation or avocation, in order to share this wisdom with others. Though I have a background in research and studied some of these very topics for my doctoral dissertation, my goal for this book is to share the compelling stories of retired CEOs' journeys so that other driven individuals may start to imagine a post-business leadership future that inspires and excites them, even if they are a long way from retirement themselves.

While many books and articles have explored risks and challenges to business and family continuity, less has been written on the importance, challenges, dimensions, and consequences of *personal* continuity. That is, how might outcomes change throughout the system if we can help driven, successful individuals imagine and plan for a post-career life of purpose including meaningful goals beyond the business objectives to which they have committed so much of their adult life and energy? In writing this book I wanted to answer an important but daunting question for such leaders: When you have anchored so much of your life around one significant role, how can you fashion new roles that will challenge you and provide you with purpose and joy?

This book will explore the topic with a simple conceptual model (described in Chapter 2) that seeks to illustrate how the individual CEO's personality and priorities in this journey will interact with the needs of the business, family, and community. The model is not meant to be predictive nor does it aspire to capture exhaustively all that goes into this process of transition; rather, I use it to provide a visual reminder of how these core pieces in a family business system all affect one another. Even more compelling, I hope, are the stories I will share along the way that bring these ideas to life in the context of real family business leaders who have been down this path.

Moreover, I hope to help readers understand that late-life roles and purposes may take many different shapes, none better than the other – as long as it is authentic to the individual involved. Some of the personal continuity stories here capture aggressive new directions, such as starting up new enterprises; some include more behind-the-scenes roles, including mentoring business/board leaders; still others reflect the spiritual or reflective domain, such as drafting a memoir or engaging in meaningful service work.

There are many paths to joy and fulfillment. My hope is that the ideas and examples in this book will inspire and motivate others to engage in planning their own "Next" with resolve, understanding, and intention.

Chicago, Illinois, United States   Stephanie Brun de Pontet

Acknowledgements

This book wouldn't have been possible without the valuable contributions and support of many people.

First, I want to express my deepest appreciation to the 13 extraordinary family business leaders who willingly offered to be interviewed for this book. Each was motivated to make a difference by sharing their journey and wisdom, to help others navigate this major life transition. Your stories were an inspiration, and your contributions are the heart of this book.

Further ideas and inspiration emerged from what I learn daily from clients and colleagues committed to the hard work of doing 'the right thing' in all spheres they touch. It's a privilege to work alongside such thoughtful client families, and to support their diverse journeys. Special thanks, too, to the full FBCG team, who provided valuable feedback on elements of this book – in particular to Otis Baskin, who provided feedback on manuscript drafts, and to Karen King, who was a vital sounding board for the visuals.

A project of this scale requires a dedicated team, and I am fortunate to have had a great group of hands-on collaborators. Special thanks to Sachin Waikar, who worked closely with me to bring this book together, sharing ideas, reviewing and refining content, and providing much-needed encouragement at every stage. Thanks also to Michael Mok and Ashley Gerou, who did a terrific job on graphics and cover design, respectively. A special note of gratitude to Marcus Ballenger and the entire Palgrave-Macmillan team, who worked tirelessly to get this book produced and out into the world.

While I am fortunate to have had the support of so many professionals in this effort, I would be remiss if I did not acknowledge the family that stands behind me in all my pursuits. First, my mother Joan, who is an extraordinary model of dedication to both family and work – having achieved great success in both – and who has made her own transition from the top with grace. Second, my partner Jim, an entrepreneur who has made – and continues to make – big sacrifices in pursuit of building a business that can make a real difference in the world. Sharing this journey with him has deepened my appreciation for the vision, passion, and intrinsic reward that motivates this kind of focus and commitment among effective leaders. And finally, my daughters Gabrielle and Ariane, who experience directly the sacrifices that a parent makes when she is likely over-committed to her professional pursuits. My hope is they learn the value of pursuing a professional path that can motivate this kind of passion and joy – and that they can teach me how to achieve a better balance going forward!

Contents

1 Introduction 1

2 Conceptual Model 13

3 Beware the Identity Trap 23

4 How Ready Are You for Change? 39

5 Is Your Family Ready for Your Transition? 61

6 Is Your Business Ready for Your Transition? 81

7 Where Are You From and Why Does That Matter? 99

8 Where Do You Want to Go (and How Do You Know?) 113

9 Get Around Roadblocks, Assess Your Readiness, and Keep Score 135

10 Conclusion 149

Appendix 1: Brief Interviewee Profiles   155

Appendix 2: Interview Questions   169

Appendix 3: Scoring Guides for Assessment Tools   173

Recommended Readings and Other Resources   189

Index   193

List of Figures

Fig. 2.1	Conceptual model	14
Fig. 3.1	Personal readiness	24
Fig. 4.1	Personal readiness	40
Fig. 5.1	Family readiness	62
Fig. 6.1	Business readiness	82
Fig. 7.1	Conceptual model	100

List of Tables

Table 3.1	Centrality of Work Role	33
Table 3.2	Role Allocation	36
Table 4.1	General Readiness for Change	41
Table 4.2	Openness to Experience	43
Table 4.3	Desire for Control	47
Table 4.4	Servant Leadership Style	48
Table 4.5	Capacity for Disengagement and Reengagement	52
Table 4.6	Staying Engaged Despite Health Limitations	55
Table 5.1	Talk Through 'Retirement' with Your Partner	66
Table 5.2	Questions to Strengthen Your Relationship	68
Table 5.3	Manage the Togetherness-Individuality Paradox with Care	74
Table 5.4	Assessing Family Stakeholder Readiness	78
Table 5.5	Tips on a 'Reset' to Strengthen Family Bonds	79
Table 6.1	How Ready is Your Business for Transition?	96
Table 6.2	Confidence in Prospective Successor	97
Table 7.1	Combat Ageism!	110
Table 8.1	Importance of Impact	117
Table 8.2	Individual Drivers	129
Table 9.1	Talk About Competing Needs	142
Table 9.2	Plan for Your Plan	143
Table 9.3	Overall Readiness Assessment	145

1

Introduction

Dick DeVos is soaring in retirement. In 2010, the past leader of direct-selling giant Amway combined his passions for flying and education to found the West Michigan Aviation Academy, an airport-based four-year high school—just one of the former company president's many post-career pursuits. "We have 600 students today," DeVos explains, "and provide kids with a great education strong in aviation, robotics and engineering." Many students advance to flying solo and earning their pilot's licenses, opening up multiple career opportunities.

Dick is a great example of a former family business leader who has found fulfillment post-retirement by using his interests to identify and work on meaningful projects. While many former leaders have followed similar paths, others report much less positive post-work experiences as they struggle with loss of identity and meaning. "I had observed people retiring … and then a year later they would drop dead and that was not how I wanted things to go," says Frank Schurz, former CEO of Schurz Communications, which had hundreds of millions in revenue at its peak. Inspired by these observations to think ahead, Frank pursued passions for fishing and water-fowl hunting while still working. "I figured once you retire you can convert this hobby into a passion and then eventually to a total compulsion," he continues. That's exactly what he did, from becoming part owner of a fishing lodge to joining several conservation organizations, making great friends along the way.

There are countless other positive and negative examples of family business leaders making the transition to post-work life. This book is about how better to make that change, with the goal of not just letting go of the leadership role that likely occupied decades of your life, but of finding true fulfillment in "life after work." Success with this transition requires proactive planning for multiple dimensions of your "personal continuity," as we'll discuss.

In many ways, the first step to planning ahead is to understand that any leadership transition happens within multiple systems, and thus represents more than a one-time, clearly defined event.

What Succession Planning Misses

A leader's transition out of a family firm is much more than a one-time succession, or a handover between the outgoing and incoming leader. As Jim Ethier, former chairman and CEO of Bush Brothers & Company, the Tennessee-based food-processing business famous for its baked beans, states, "I wanted to build an organization. Now I am satisfied that it is done, and I have the right people in place."

Jim went on to speak about the many changes he had championed in the business and its governance, including helping the family develop an ownership vision for the future, creating governance processes and systems that would support that vision, and ensuring family members were appropriately groomed and challenged to be able to effectively step into key leadership roles.

Jim's efforts speak to the idea that a family business is not just a business but a highly complex *system*. In fact, those of us who live and study family enterprise are always deepening our understanding of how complicated this system can be, with overlapping sub-systems related to family, business, and governance. One outcome of our growing appreciation for family business's complexity has been a shift in describing "succession planning" more as "continuity planning." This seemingly subtle change reflects our realization that leadership transition affects much more than the two individuals changing roles—it's never just about *one* succession—and that this top-level change will have strong impact on the continuity and functioning of the entire enterprise and all its constituents, or stakeholders.[1] Moreover, as "continuity" has an active and positive tone, it combats the resistance many CEOs have to talking about retirement or "succession," which feels to some like a thinly veiled term for their imminent departure.

I have a friend who is clear on this topic, he says: 'we don't use the R-word around here.'

JACK CAKEBREAD, FOUNDER AND HONORARY CHAIRMAN OF CAKEBREAD CELLARS (REFERRING TO A FRIEND DISCUSSING RETIREMENT)

Part of the challenge is that while there's a lot of thinking on how family business systems and stakeholders may need to evolve to support the continuity of the enterprising family and operating business,[2] there's little consideration of the *personal continuity* of a leader transitioning out of their role. Many books and articles have addressed the topic of the CEO's resistance to "letting go," but almost nothing has been said about how these individuals might continue to contribute in a meaningful way once they've exited business leadership, creating benefits not only for themselves but also their family, business, and broader community.

Another way to think about this important issue is to ask: *Why would healthy, capable and driven people let go of a powerful role they enjoy if they have nothing to move toward afterward?* Indeed, this book's premise is that lack of clarity or options for meaningful post-CEO roles is a major factor in succession struggles, and can have wider-reaching negative consequences on the family, business, and other systems in which the departing leader is based.

The good news is that retiring leaders can use their passions—including those discovered while running their family business—to guide their post-career decisions and activities, as we'll discuss at length later in the book. The words of Phil Clemens, former CEO of Pennsylvania-based Clemens Family Corporation, which holds food businesses including Hatfield Quality Meats, exemplify this idea.

I don't want to accept money to help people [as a retiree]. I mentor people because it's a passion. I have a passion to promote healthy families and healthy family businesses and healthy non-profits, so that is where I invest my time.

PHIL CLEMENS, FORMER CEO OF CLEMENS FAMILY CORPORATION

His post-work life involves serving on the boards of several organizations, including corporations, non-profits, and Christian colleges.

What the Research Found

My interest in the topic of personal continuity may have originated in my observations of my grandfathers' histories (see Preface), but has deepened considerably through my work with family businesses and the research I pursued on retiring family business CEOs for my doctoral thesis in psychology.[3] My study, which followed retiring family business leaders over three years, found that leaders with a greater capacity for reengagement—defined as the ability to find and commit to *new* goals when a valued goal must be abandoned (see Chapter 4 for more details)—had taken more concrete steps toward retirement planning across domains than those for whom reengagement was inherently more difficult. Unsurprisingly, concrete planning by the outgoing CEO also led to better outcomes for the business.

My study also found that outgoing CEOs felt like they were conceding or sharing more authority than successors felt they were gaining. The classic example of this is the "retiring" CEO who feels that they are increasingly releasing control by spending more time in Florida or some other sunny locale, away from the business, while still calling in to work daily, countering decisions the new leadership team has made, and actively directing team members. Not surprisingly, rising successors in this context do not feel they have much in the way of real, new authority, so they tend to describe the "shift" in authority very differently than the outgoing leader would. These differences in perception can clearly be sources of conflict. The implication of this is that understanding the challenge and struggling with the question of what comes next for the departing leader may build empathy and better outcomes for *everyone* in the system.

Another interesting result from the study was that incumbent leaders who have an easier time disengaging, or letting go, are less likely to escalate commitment to their leadership role in the face of declining business performance, which helps them make the transition to post-work life. Not surprisingly, I also found a link between active planning for retirement and the ability to commit to new goals. Like any new, important undertaking, creating a fulfilling post-work life needs some level of intentional planning.

In the interviews for this book, when I asked retired CEOs about their non-work-related commitments, it was evident that strong passions and outside interests created a natural platform for ongoing purpose and general fulfillment in their post-leadership life. For example, many talked about their lifelong engagement with faith-based organizations, and most had substantial interests in more than one outside-of-work commitment: former family business leaders Dick DeVos and Phil Clemens, both mentioned earlier, have pursued leadership with multiple faith-based educational organizations, for instance.

Themes of This Book

While my research helped me to identify the many factors that go into personal continuity, this book is anchored firmly in the *application* of research from years of consulting, and the rich stories of CEOs and other key business leaders who have successfully transitioned from their leadership role to a truly satisfying post-primary career life. My goal with this book is twofold:

- To highlight real-life models of success who can provide ideas and inspiration to others facing challenges related to personal continuity;
- To educate and help *all* in the system appreciate why this transition is often more complicated than expected.

To serve these ends, I will cover the themes below in depth.

CEO Transitions Never Happen in a Vacuum

There's significant interplay between the personal "state of readiness" of the individual CEO in transition and the systems this change will touch, including family, business, and broader community, each of which has multiple elements. This interaction among multiple systems is the heart of the conceptual model I will explain more fully in Chapter 2.

Change Is Hard; This Particular Change Is *Really* Hard

It is human nature to resist change because the uncertainty that comes with the unknown almost always causes stress and discomfort.[4] Further, leaving the role of CEO or chairman is a change that involves a significant loss of identity or sense of self for most, as well as a reduction in perceived prestige and actual power.[5] These losses represent a real cost to the person in transition. Change related to personal continuity in a family business context is also made harder because of the complex interaction of systems—family, business, governance, community—involved, as mentioned earlier.

Humans Are Purpose Driven

It is well-accepted that humans need direction and purpose in life to feel truly fulfilled. This is true over the entire lifespan; so, as you get older, even if you've accomplished a lot, you'll still search for direction and purpose to give your life meaning. In some ways, older adults have a particularly strong need to feel they have ongoing relevance, as they have already completed their active tenures in roles such as parent and professional.[6] Moreover, retirement leads to drastic changes in three key areas for anyone: identity, relationships, purpose.[7]

This may help us understand why a future imagined to include only travel and leisure does not feel sufficient or motivating to many, especially those who have enjoyed success in the business world or other domains. Lack of purpose is of concern not only for the individual in question but also broader society, as Marc Freedman suggests in describing "a worrisome dystopian scenario … in which the largest segment of society [senior citizens] is at loose ends, and under engaged."[8] He also asks, "Does it make much sense for society to throw away the most experienced segment of the population when it is a long way from obsolescence?"[9] As such, lack of vision around a purpose beyond retirement may have far-reaching effects.

I know what I am not going to do. I am not going to go play golf every day. I have ideas about some mentoring, teaching, and non-profit work, and I may even write a book.

IRV ROBINSON, CO-FOUNDER AND FORMER CEO OF PACKAGING COMPANY ROBBIE FANTASTIC

Personal Continuity Planning Is Important But Rarely Undertaken

"If you don't know where you are going, any road will get you there," says the old adage. Successful business leaders understand that significant business changes require planning. But they may fail to recognize that what is true for the enterprise is also true for the *individual*. Just as the business may face a series of simultaneous changes as a generational transition looms (entering new markets, greater professionalization of management, increased number of shareholders, and others), the individual leader transitioning to retirement may also be experiencing a range of personal changes (move to a different house, health issues, greater number of grandchildren, and the like). Given this complexity and the increasing number of post-retirement years in developed countries, it is surprising how little planning individuals typically do for this phase of life. For example, a survey of recent retirees found that 62% had retired without *any idea* of how they would craft a life or adjust to retirement; the trend has prompted experts to point out that many people spend more time planning a wedding than planning for retirement.[10] Finally, as a sense of loss of control is particularly stressful to Type-A CEOs,[11] exerting some control over the situation through effective and intentional planning may be particularly important.

Stories of Success ("It Can Be Done")

While well-researched theories may be intellectually stimulating, most of us learn and retain information better through stories. Several recently retired

CEOs generously agreed to be interviewed for this book (the list of interviewees is shared later in this chapter); their stories illustrate the challenges and triumphs that are part of this journey. The goal in sharing these examples of success is to provide guidance, wisdom, and ideas from the experience of real business leaders. I hope these stories will endow you with inspiration that there is a compelling path to be found beyond the role of CEO, as well as some specific ideas for how to find the right path for you.

Who Will Benefit from This Book?

As described earlier, this book's goal is to help explain why a family business leader's transition to a fulfilling post-work life can be so challenging, and to provide examples and ideas for success, along with specific, practical insights and advice in the form of frameworks, tools, and other resources. The book is meant to help retiring CEOs and others in the systems they inhabit experience a much smoother, more effective journey and outcome, leading to greater satisfaction and fulfillment for all.

In this context, specific audiences for the book include:

- *Family business or entrepreneurial CEOs*, who can gain greater self-knowledge and planning guidance;
- *Family members of transitioning business leaders*, who can gain empathy for those in transition and help them plan for the entire system's benefit;
- *Business executives, partners, and board members of the business in question*, who can also gain empathy for those undergoing the process and provide meaningful support for planning and adjustment;
- *Advisors to business owners*, who can gain heightened awareness of issues and options related to continuity planning and provide advice and support for the planning process;
- *Students of family business and/or leadership succession*, who can gain awareness of key issues in preparation for leadership transitions in which they may have a role—and their own eventual transitions.

How the Book Is Structured (and Whom I Interviewed)

The book includes the following sections.

Section One: Introduction

The first two chapters, including this one, describe why the topic of personal continuity is important, complicated, and poorly understood. This chapter has already covered some relevant background research, including my own. Chapter 2 presents the conceptual model for personal continuity—including the core concept of personal readiness—on which the book is based.

Section Two: Internal Readiness

Chapters 3 and 4 detail what I consider the *internal* component of the conceptual model. Major ideas and themes covered include:

- How central your professional role is to your overall sense of identity;
- How difficult (or easy) it may be for you to make significant changes;
- The role of your physical and emotional health and resilience.

Section Three: System Readiness and Broader Context

Chapters 5, 6, and 7 examine the *external* elements of the conceptual model, specifically considering the role and situation of your family and business, as well as the broader context in which all of this plays out. Major ideas and themes include:

- The strength and nature of your key relationships (spouse, children, colleagues, and others);
- The stability and structures of the business (has it evolved adequately, for example, to support the transition?);
- The strength and relevance of your community networks;
- How your cultural context might affect the transition.

Section Four: Planning Your Path Forward and Conclusion

Chapters 8, 9, and 10 provide concrete guidance on how to imagine and plan for the next phase of your life. Key ideas covered include:

- How to translate your skills, passions, and experience into future opportunities;
- The importance of concrete yet flexible planning;
- Defining measures of success that you can track;

- Understanding and overcoming common roadblocks;
- Tying together all the key themes and recommendations from the book.

Stories, Tips, and Tools (Throughout the Book)

The material in this book comes to life thanks to the compelling stories shared by CEOs and other family business leaders who have made the challenging journey from active day-to-day leadership of their enterprise to the pursuit of new challenges and passions that energize and motivate them. Most of these stories were collected via telephone interviews (see Appendix 2 for interview script), though some were related through in-person visits.

How did I choose the CEOs interviewed? I selected them from a broad network of contacts as examples of individuals who have achieved demonstrable success with this difficult transition. In particular, I looked to speak with former family business leaders who are continuing to engage in the world in personally meaningful ways—whether through hobbies, volunteer work, grandparenting, new business ventures, travel, faith-related service, board service, civic engagement, mentoring, and others. I recognize that the notion of "successful" retirement is inherently subjective; my primary interest was in connecting with individuals who feel fulfilled with the life they have built for themselves at this new stage in their personal journey.

Conducting these interviews was tremendously rewarding in its own right. I feel deeply privileged to have heard such a diverse set of stories from compelling and thoughtful leaders who were so generous with their time for this project. I could have kept interviewing more and more leaders in my network and beyond—and would have loved to have had a few more women leaders in this sample—but at a certain point, you have to stop gathering information and start the hard work of writing! While having only one retired woman CEO who participated directly as an interviewee for this book is no doubt a limitation of perspectives, there is some counter-balance, as certainly my thinking is influenced by my own gender as well as the experiences and perspectives of the many female business leaders with whom I have worked over the years. With that caveat and appreciation, here are the leaders interviewed for the book (I have included a very short bio on each in Appendix 1 as well).

- Eric Allyn, past co-chairman of Welch Allyn, a global enterprise which develops and manufactures medical devices.
- Murray Berstein, founder and former CEO of Nixon Uniform Service and Medical Wear, a company serving 7000 practices throughout the mid-Atlantic and North East.

- Jack Cakebread, founder and honorary chairman of premier winery Cakebread Cellars.
- Marilyn Carlson Nelson, former chair and CEO of global travel, hospitality and marketing company, Carlson.
- Phil Clemens, former CEO of the Clemens Family Corporation, which holds multiple specialty food businesses.
- Lanse Crane, former CEO of Crane & Company, which offers a wide range of products including the paper on which US currency is printed.
- Dick DeVos, former president of global direct-selling company Amway.
- Jim Ethier, former chairman and CEO of Bush Brothers & Company, the USA's leading producer of branded bean products.
- David Geller, co-founder and CEO of JOYN (formerly GV Financial), an independent registered advisory firm, specializing in behavioral wealth management.
- Jack Herschend, former CEO of Herschend Entertainment, which operates amusement parks and other entertainment attractions such as the Harlem Globe Trotters.
- David Juday, former CEO of test and measurement equipment company Ideal Industries, providing distribution of products for professional electricians for more than 100 years.
- Irv Robinson, co-founder and former CEO of plastic and packaging company Robbie Manufacturing, inc., doing business as "Robbie Fantastic Flexibles."
- Frank Schurz, former CEO of Schurz Communication, a holding company that owns a number of cable and publishing companies.

The goal of highlighting success stories is to provide readers with the idea that post-work life can be meaningful and productive, and also to illustrate a broad spectrum of paths that could resonate for them as well. While my approach is not scientific in the same sense that my academic research has been, the rich anecdotes provided by my interviewees provide important takeaways for those in, or soon to be in similar shoes.

In addition to the many examples, the book offers numerous assessment tools and specific tips throughout to support readers in their own journeys. Some of these instruments are 'simplified' versions of scales or tools that are sometimes used in research, and others I created based on my knowledge and reading in this field, to provoke thinking. Here again I caution readers not to see the tools provided as scientific or comprehensive; rather, they are meant as conversation starters or simple ways to help you identify patterns, insights, and potential gaps related to the context of your transition, including your mindset and factors in the systems surrounding you.

While each person's journey is unique, I hope you find the material here helpful in your own transition, whatever form it takes.

Notes

1. See, for example, Randel Carlock and John L. Ward, *When Family Businesses are Best: The Parallel Planning Process for Family Harmony and Business Success* (Palgrave Macmillan, New York, 2010).
2. See, for example, Kelly Lecouvie and Jennifer Pendergast, *Family Business Succession: Your Roadmap to Continuity* (Palgrave Macmillan, New York, 2014), for detailed thinking on challenges and opportunities related to succession.
3. Stephanie Brun de Pontet. *Using theories of control and self-regulation to examine the leadership transition between a parent and child in family-owned businesses.* Unpublished doctoral dissertation, Concordia University, 2008.
4. A great book on the general topic of change and transition is William Bridges and Susan Bridges, *Managing Transitions* (Da Capo, Philadelphia, 2009).
5. See, for example, Manfred F.R. Kets de Vries, "The Many Colors of Success: What do Executives Want out of Life?" *Organizational Dynamics*, 2009, 39(1), pp. 1–12.
6. See, for example, George Vaillant, *Aging Well* (Little, Brown and Co., Boston, 2002).
7. Nancy Schlossberg, *Revitalizing Retirement: Reshaping your Identity, Relationships, and Purpose* (American Psychological Association, Washington, DC, 2009).
8. Marc Freedman, *The Big Shift: Navigating the New Stage Beyond Midlife*, Hachette, 2012, p. 169.
9. Marc Freedman, *The Big Shift: Navigating the New Stage Beyond Midlife*, Hachette, 2012, p. 14.
10. As noted in Nancy Schlossberg, *Revitalizing Retirement: Reshaping your Identity, Relationships, and Purpose* (American Psychological Association, Washington, DC, 2009).
11. Harry Levinson and Jerry Wofford, "Approaching Retirement as the Flexibility Phase," *Academy of Management Executive*, May 2000, 14(2), p. 84.

2

Conceptual Model

> We knew we had to manage transition on many levels. There was this tacit understanding that we wanted to own the company as a family into future generations but we didn't know what that really meant.
>
> **DAVID JUDAY,** FORMER CEO OF TEST AND EQUIPMENT COMPANY IDEAL INDUSTRIES, SPEAKING ABOUT PAST LEADERSHIP SUCCESSION.

That's a common sentiment among family businesses with top leaders in transition: they have a sense of their long-term goals but may be unsure of how best to bring those to life. That's because the transition affects an entire, complicated system, rather than just a small set of individuals. Moreover, within that system, the readiness (or lack thereof) of all the sub-parts for an impending transition are critical.

To help navigate this complexity, I've created a model of the systems and context involved in such leadership transitions. While the real world rarely resembles a conceptual model, sometimes a basic visual representation helps us see and better understand how specific elements of a system fit together and affect one another. The Personal Continuity Readiness model (see Fig. 2.1)

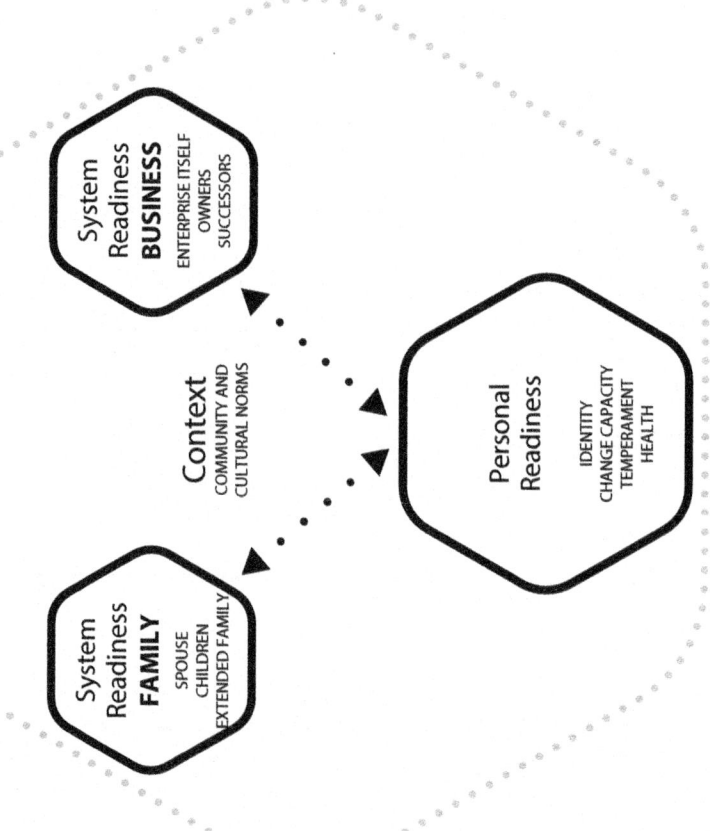

Fig. 2.1 Conceptual model

shows how the environment and context of the family business systems may influence an individual business leader's personal state of readiness to prepare for—and progress toward—a fulfilling post-business leadership life.

Now let's talk about each of the model's components.

Personal Readiness

At its core, this book is about personal continuity in the context of a transition away from business leadership. That requires a high level of personal readiness for the transitioning leader. As discussed briefly in Chapter 1, when you have achieved at high levels in your career and have served in a position of real authority and responsibility (leading your family's business, in this case), shifting away from that chapter of your life is a huge change that involves many losses: loss of position, loss of power, loss of a place to go every day, loss of helpers and other perks of business leadership, and loss of identity—to name just a few. So, it's not surprising that many individuals struggle to let go of their leadership roles. Moreover, central to this book is the idea that lack of clarity related to a positive and stimulating path forward makes an already difficult change feel almost unbearable to many of those facing this transition.

Despite the high level of challenge, some business leaders do a very good job of transitioning out of their professional role into new, purposeful directions; whereas others, in similar circumstances, make this leap only with great difficulty or fail to make it at all. In my observation of and discussions with many former business leaders, I have understood that those who struggle fall generally into two camps:

- *Failure to leave:* Leaders who never really transition; they don't ever truly let go of their role within the family business.
- *Failure to thrive:* Leaders who do a good job of absorbing widespread wisdom about "getting out of the way" of the next generation, yet fail to find the right post-work path to keep them engaged and able to contribute in a way that gives their days' clear purpose and their life deep joy. These individuals find only limited outlets for their wisdom, experience, and energy. For an example of this situation, see the "Jack's Passionless Post-Work Life" box—a story built from a composite of many struggling retired leaders I have encountered over the years.

> **Jack's Passionless Post-Work Life**
>
> Jack Smith grew a large manufacturing business in the Midwest through hard work and a sharp focus on customer service. When his two sons, who had joined the business early in their careers, attained positions of real responsibility and were looking for more, Jack sought advice to plan for a successful transition. His advisors, including attorneys and family business consultants, suggested he establish a professional board including independent directors, develop even clearer leadership opportunities and roles for his sons, and gradually reduce his involvement in daily operations. Jack took the advice seriously, and transitioned out of the business several years ago. Today, he is proud of how well his sons are leading the business, which has grown steadily. But he is miserable about his daily life.
>
> It is clear that he feels adrift. For example, he spends considerable time away from his hometown, where the business is headquartered—not because he is drawn to travel or challenges away from home but because he is afraid of getting in the way of the business. He and his wife go on global tours and cruises and spend relaxing time with fellow retired friends. Yet Jack longs for his days making strategic decisions, and guiding others in achieving goals.
>
> In short, while Jack has done a good job assuring the continuity of his company and the development of his sons as business leaders, and even successfully "let go," it's also clear he didn't invest sufficiently in his *own* continuity. Planning the next stage more carefully—serving on boards of outside businesses or non-profits, for example—might not only have led to a more fulfilling retirement for Jack and allowed him to help growing organizations but also helped him add more value to his family and business through his ongoing exposure to new ideas and opportunities.

In this context, the personal readiness part of the model represents the business leader's personal sense of readiness for the transition. While there are many individual characteristics we could consider as influences on personal readiness, four important ones I have observed are noted in the model in Fig. 2.1 and described here:

- *Identity:* How you define yourself; the roles and labels you walk around with that influence both how you see your place in the world and how others might relate to you—note that some people have fairly narrow senses of their identity (as associated with the "workaholic" stereotype, for example), while others have a broader definition including multiple roles;
- *Change capacity:* How easy or hard it is for you to let go of an important goal or pursuit and start to pursue new priorities, as would be required for a fulfilling retirement;

- *Temperament:* Your core internal "wiring"; whether you are quick to anger versus even-keeled, introverted versus expressive, fast-paced versus deliberate, and so on;
- *Health:* Your overall sense of physical and mental well-being.

These four personal readiness indicators are not meant to be an exhaustive list, but as a set, they provide good insight into why some CEOs will struggle more than others with the move to post-work life—as one or more of these factors almost always play an important role. We will take a deeper dive into how these variables play a role in personal readiness in Chaps. 3 and 4.

System Readiness

As has already been articulated here, the transition out of leadership for a family business CEO happens in the context of two significant and related systems. The extent to which each of these systems is ready for the change may impact the transitioning CEO's journey. Note also that these are *reciprocal* relationships, as suggested by the bidirectional arrows in Fig. 2.1. That is, the CEO's personal readiness also impacts the readiness of these external systems. For example, a CEO who is naturally uncomfortable with change may resist putting in place the professional management and oversight processes that the business system must develop before it can be overseen effectively by the next generation.

As a departing leader, you have to think of the entire entity before you think of yourself.

ERIC ALLYN, PAST CO-CHAIRMAN OF MEDICAL EQUIPMENT COMPANY WELCH ALLYN

At the same time, if the business is struggling to adapt to new structures of oversight and a cadre of key leaders chooses to leave the company when the CEO is considering his or her exit, this set of *business readiness* issues will almost definitely impact adversely the CEO's personal sense of security and readiness. Let's look more closely at each of the systems in the model.

Family

An individual's transition out of their professional work role and into the next phase of life will undoubtedly have an impact on their family, especially their spouse. For example, if the CEO has devoted themselves much more to the business than the family over many years, that departing leader's uncertainty about how family relationships will work once they are no longer at the office daily may increase their anxiety around the future. That situation could also lead to the failure of other immediate family members (spouse or children) to support change. On the other hand, a warm, supportive marriage with many shared interests and healthy levels of dependence/independence could serve to motivate and inspire ideas for new, shared opportunities in this next phase of life's journey, as is true for families facing *any* kind of transition.

In addition, the needs and expectations of children and grandchildren may play a role in shaping this phase of your life. For instance, if there is hope that as the parents move into retirement they would be more available to help with grandchildren, this may serve to motivate or demotivate the transition for the CEO. Further, in the context of a family business, a broader set of family stakeholders could be impacted directly by this change, and their readiness may affect the CEO's frame of mind around the transition as well. For example, if the CEO has children, nieces, or nephews who have—or may come into—ownership of the business, these shareholders may resist the CEO's leaving the leadership post, as they could worry that the next leader will not do as good a job as their predecessor, or may not communicate with them or support them as consistently. Chapter 5 will explore these themes in greater detail.

Business

In addition to the preparation and capabilities of the incoming leader, if the business has not developed the structures it needs to support the CEO's exit, it may preclude even the most retirement-oriented leader from departing, and may also limit his or her bandwidth in developing outside interests, connections, and passions that could give purpose to their next phase. There is of course an interplay with the CEO's personal readiness here. A CEO whose identity is wrapped up in this professional role (or who is temperamentally uncomfortable with change) may perceive that the team around him or her is not ready when in fact they may well be by all objective measures.

Moreover, just as family members' personal concerns about the exit of the CEO may lead them to oppose or adversely impact this process, the same is true of the executive leadership team. The case we often see is a cadre of senior leaders, whether family members or not, who "grew up" in the business with the current CEO, worried that the departure of their mentor may reduce their own authority or role in the system. Their concerns may lead them to resist actively the changes needed for a smooth transition. Chapter 6 discusses these types of issues in greater depth.

Context

While not a distinct system like the business or family system, the context in which a leader's transition unfolds typically has genuine impact on the options considered and opportunities available. The broader personal network of the outgoing CEO is one aspect of context that may play a role in their transition in a variety of ways. Humans are social creatures and most of us need friends and other social contacts in addition to our family ties. Some driven business leaders have limited social relations outside of work because of the time they have devoted to their professional role, or they may live in a small community where they do not have many peers with similar interests and experience. But others have very strong networks, in part because their visible role as a business leader has opened doors over the years and provided an entry to organizations, clubs, or associations where further relationships and connections have evolved.

It can certainly be the case that a CEO has plenty of friends and social acquaintances, and many business leaders are in this position. But it's fair to ask how many of these relationships are anchored around the leader's role. For example, if most of the people with whom you socialize are business colleagues, suppliers, or industry players, how will those ties evolve, or dissolve, once you leave the CEO post? In some cases, the relationships weather the transition well, as the personal relationship is deeper than the business connection. In other situations, however, leaving the CEO role may diminish your contact with others, or erode the relevance of these ties, potentially contributing to feelings of isolation for you.

In addition to the emotional toll associated with potential loss of relationships, there is a practical side to these networks as well, as they relate directly to helping the departing CEO gain access to post-work opportunities which they may find engaging. A person who is looking to discover ways to contribute outside of the business where they have long played a role needs access to decision-makers, organizations, or partners who can open doors or collaborate with them on new activities or adventures.

> I have always believed that business can be a powerful force for good. It creates jobs, fulfills needs, and brings diverse people together around common objectives and funds the causes we are most about. The business leader carries this knowledge of how to make a positive difference within them long after they leave their titles behind. Redirecting this drive to achieve objectives outside of the company broadens your relationships and interests and in turn will open doors for you to continue to be a powerful source for good in retirement.
>
> **MARILYN CARLSON NELSON,** FORMER CHAIR AND CEO OF CARLSON

For example, when Irv Robinson was starting to think about his future transition from leadership of Robbie Fantastic Flexibles, he was able to leverage community foundation ties he'd nurtured in his town through years of philanthropy and civic engagement. He and several business friends had a community service idea of creating meaningful summer internships for disadvantaged youth, but they needed back-end and administrative support to bring the project to life. The credibility he had built over years of contact with key decision-makers in the community enabled him to enlist the backing he needed from them, which in turn allowed him to focus on what he terms the "fun stuff" related to building the initiative. Chapter 7 will provide more details on the role of networks in this process, as well as insight into how to build or broaden your network.

Social and Cultural Context

As suggested in Fig. 2.1, the individual CEO or business owner, their family and the family business all exist within a broader social and cultural context that also plays a role in the ease and nature of their transition. For example, one factor that may have a big impact on networks and other aspects of our model is the *size of the enterprise* you are leaving, as well as the *size of the community* in which you live and work. Thus, a business leader from a very prominent company or family may find that doors are more easily opened for him or her simply by virtue of name, reputation, or association. Still, not everyone will have equal access to the opportunity to serve on the board of the Cleveland Clinic, or other prestigious organizations, no matter how skilled a networker you are, nor how passionately you believe in the mission. But even hailing from a modest-sized business in a smaller city may give you access to the vast majority of local decision-makers, making it easier for you to find and plug into opportunities to contribute, using your skills and resources.

The size of locale or population density of the region may also impact *how close family members live to one another*, which is another factor influencing personal readiness and the transition. It may be more typical for families that grew up in a big city in the northeastern USA, for example, to scatter around the country, whereas folks growing up in rural Texas may prefer to stay closer to home, which may in turn influence elements of the CEO's transition, such as opportunities to spend time with extended family, including grandchildren. Obviously, this is a gross generalization, but my point is that the place from which you come impacts your values and preferences on a range of matters that will likely have some bearing on how your transition plays out.

Another context-related aspect that can play a role is the *age* at which one embarks on this transitional journey. Not only might age affect your physical health and energy (internal processes), but it may open some doors and close others with respect to new opportunities. In relation to this, one challenge in particular may arise if you would like to serve on boards. Many private company boards have age limits that might preclude this option if you are in your late 70s or older, no matter how sharp or current your business perspective and insights. Beyond board service, it can sometimes be difficult to start new opportunities of any kind in later life due to biases related to ageism.[1] Decision-makers may assume you would struggle to learn new skills or wouldn't have the energy to contribute at the level required, even if you have a well-known track record of success in your prior role.

As a final note, related to cultural context, I acknowledge this book is written with a North American bias, as that is my own cultural background, and that of the CEOs I interviewed; all were from the USA, and all but one were male. So, it's best to keep in mind that North American culture is quite *individualistic* (expectations that people will focus on individual goals and values, rather than community-oriented ones), whereas other cultures (for example, several in Asia, including China) tend to be more communal. It is fair to expect that this contextual difference would also have a bearing on this entire process. Chapter 7 will explore further the role of social and cultural context on our model.

Note

1. Ageism is a common, growing problem, especially for members of the US Baby Boomer population; that includes many transitioning family business leaders. For more, see Patricia Reaney, "Ageism in U.S. Workforce: A Persistent Problem Unlikely to Go Away," *Reuters*, October 19, 2015, http://www.reuters.com/article/us-employment-discrimination-age-idUSKCN0SD1Z720151019 (accessed January 25, 2016).

3

Beware the Identity Trap

One way or another, most people in transition have the experience of no longer being quite sure of who they are
—William Bridges, *Transitions: Making Sense of Life's Changes*[1]

"If I don't redefine myself I will go crazy," claims Eric Allyn, former executive and co-chair of medical equipment business Welch Allyn, recalling what he told himself when leaving his leadership role at the family firm after a long career devoted to his family's business. He went on:

"When I worked, I worked pretty intensely. So, it took some real self-awareness and confidence to think about how to replace that. But I was excited to help our family figure out how to become great owners, rather than the operators of the business. Still, it was really hard to think of myself not as the operator but as an owner and board member."

Allyn's words should resonate with any family business leader in transition. We spend much of our formative years in adolescence and early adulthood figuring out who we want to be and building an identity around that, as this informs life choices on multiple dimensions, and helps us to set and pursue meaningful goals. In North American culture, our work role is often the most central part of this identity. As a result, retirement, or the loss of that core identity element, can represent a genuine threat to our sense of self, and can be a very disorienting experience for many. This chapter helps you understand the impact of the transition to post-work life on identity, and why falling into an "identity trap" can make this shift so difficult, along with ways of combating the problem, as hinted at in Allyn's statement.

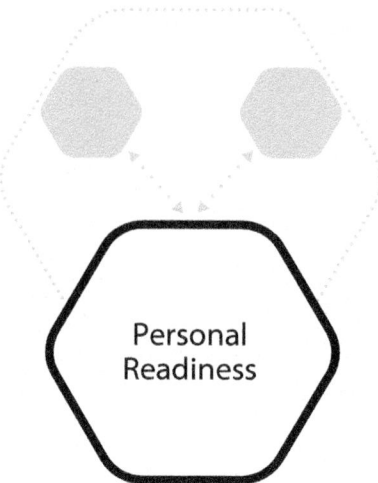

Fig. 3.1 Personal readiness

The Identity Trap

Each of us plays a variety of roles in life (e.g., daughter, mother, entrepreneur, friend, volunteer) that influence how we spend our time, how others see us and, crucially, how we see ourselves. Popular books such as Stephen Covey's excellent *The Seven Habits of Highly Effective People*, encourage us to consider *all* our roles and ensure we are investing time in the important priorities for each.[2] But in reality, many of us struggle to apply this practical wisdom consistently. In particular, ambitious and successful people tend to invest a significant percentage of their time and energy in the execution and development of their professional role. For example, a recent Gallup poll showed that people in the USA work an average of 47 hours per week—nearly a full day longer than the "40-hour" work week considered a full-time schedule—and that 40% of us work 50 or more hours per week.[3] This makes us more likely to fall into what I call an "identity trap," where your career role comes to define too much of your identity, making it difficult to move comfortably into retirement.

Family business is a common context for a sharp focus on work. In fact, in many cases, this kind of over-commitment may be required to earn the position of CEO and create the significant value so many family business leaders deliver to shareholders. Further, those successes may bring the individual great satisfaction—in addition to enabling them to build a company, create jobs, and increase their family's wealth. So, it's overly simplistic to suggest that extensive allocation of time, passion, and energy to one role to the detriment of others is something to be avoided wholesale. If that were the case, the Olympics and professional sports would not exist, or would at least showcase much less impressive displays of athleticism! Focused passion and ambition are powerful and compelling forces that, in many ways, are the engine behind our successful and innovative economy. Yet, it is important to be aware that this same laser focus may complicate your transition away from your professional role for a number of important reasons that underlie the identity trap, as discussed in the sections that follow.

Retirement Is a Challenging Transition for Many

As alluded to in Chaps. 1 and 2, several factors converge to make retirement one of life's most difficult transitions: Professionals spend the bulk of their waking hours at work pursuing responsibilities for which they have typically gained a great deal of experience and skills; work structures our days and enables us to feel validated and impactful; retirement from a valued career represents a life transition that affects deeply your sense of who you are, your relationships, and your sense of purpose. It is clear, then, that many professionals may consciously or unconsciously avoid addressing the topic of retirement, because they recognize at some level how fundamental work is to their life and identity. This is consistent with what we often see as advisors to family businesses, where incumbent CEOs may actively resist any planning conversations that would require confrontation with their eventual retirement.

Any Role Loss Is Hard: Especially When the Role Is Central to Your Identity

When one of the roles we play in life is central to our sense of self, the loss of that role for any reason can lead us to feel adrift and without purpose or value. If 80% or more of your waking hours are consumed with doing one thing and being one person (the boss, an elite athlete, mom), when the time comes for you to relinquish that role in whole or in large part, it may lead to a tremendous sense of emptiness, confusion, or lack of direction.[4] Individuals in this situation may struggle with a sense of not knowing who they are any more—a disorienting feeling, to say the least.

> Loss of power is real. For me I don't feel I add value anymore, and emotionally that is probably the biggest thing that hits me.
>
> **MURRAY BERSTEIN,** FOUNDER AND FORMER CEO OF NIXON UNIFORM SERVICE & MEDICAL WEAR

This is especially the case for work-related roles. When role loss comes through retirement, there is evidence that the more central your job is to your sense of self, the more negative your expectations for what life will be like in retirement, which can then become a self-fulfilling prophecy (or a case where believing something makes it more likely to come true).[5] It's no wonder surveys have found that loss of identity is the number one fear of retirees.[6] This may be even more pronounced in the case of family business CEOs, who often have a strong sense of professional pride and engagement with their work/position, in addition to a family connection to the history and legacy of the business, thus making this role even more central to their overall sense of self.

Beyond the centrality of a role like family business CEO to an individual's identity, this job typically consumes a great deal of time and likely has required extensive commitment and sacrifice over the years to attain. As an example, CEOs of major public companies report routinely waking at 5:00 a.m. or even earlier to start work, and not ending their work days until well into the evening, thus clocking 12- to 16-hour days and often working on weekends as well.[7] The same is true for many family business leaders, in my observation. The natural result is that the CEO may have had less opportunity to develop or strengthen other roles or facets of their life, whether related to family, friendships, or personal pursuits. This means that more of their identity is allocated to just one basket (career), which may help explain why the loss of this role feels so emotionally costly.

While every leader's specific path and workload will vary, it's clear that a family business leadership role can be all-consuming. When a role is so central to your identity, it may be very hard for you even to imagine a different way of life, different routine or schedule, and different contributors to identity.[8] In short, the "I'm no longer CEO" phase of life can be virtually impossible for you to imagine, and thus very difficult to plan for effectively—how can we plan for a future we can't envision?

Loss of Benefits and Status

While loss of one's central identity is certainly a major challenge in this situation, there are a number of additional, more practical losses that come with the end of the leadership role and may contribute further to the challenge CEOs have with their transition. Specifically, positions of leadership at work often come with perks, authority, privilege, and status that may not be readily available in retirement, representing further costs of movement into the post-work stage. Here are several of the most prominent ones.

Office and Administrative Support

Typically, CEOs have a nice office arrangement, as well as a capable administrative staff that knows them well, and may have long provided *personal* administrative help in addition to assisting with CEO/business-specific tasks. Today's retiring leader may retain a board position or have other professional responsibilities that will continue past their tenure in this role, and rightly worry about how they will get the administrative support they may need to be effective going forward. Below is an example of this sentiment from an outgoing family business leader to whom I was providing some consulting support during his transition process.

> I am not sure what I will do without Sarah [executive assistant]. She has managed my calendar and expenses and organized my travel for the past 20 years. While I am sure I could handle these tasks, it feels a bit daunting. On top of that, while I want to clear out of here to ensure there is no confusion about who is in charge, I am really not sure what I will do with all my files. I have years of notes, board minutes, industry information – documents I am used to having nearby and that I may need for my board work here and elsewhere.
>
> *RETIRING CEO OF MIDWEST MANUFACTURING BUSINESS*

Decision-Making Authority

When you represent the "here" in the "buck stops here," the idea that decisions will continue to get made without your input or guidance can be hard to swallow. While a retiring leader may understand rationally that someone else is going to be stepping into that role and making those decisions going forward, grasping that in the abstract and accepting it emotionally can be very different matters. Obviously, the retiring CEO wants their successor to succeed and be effective, yet it is very natural to have some ambivalence about the company's ability to continue and thrive when you are no longer at the helm.

> That was one of the biggest surprises to me. While I was glad that 'Jane' and her team felt confident making key decisions on their own – and I am proud to say they've had great success in doing so – I had to fight feeling hurt every time they made an important decision without my input.
>
> RETIRED CEO OF MULTI-LOCATION RETAIL SERVICE COMPANY IN SOUTHEAST

Access to Perks

In addition to an office, meeting space, and administrative support, many CEOs enjoy access to transportation, a large entertainment-expense account, high-end health benefits, and myriad other perks that support their work responsibilities, are considered part of their total compensation, or both. The classic example is access to the company jet or to a car and driver. While a retiring CEO likely understands that they will get to fly on the company plane far less often, this change in their travel realities is another of many adjustments that come with the loss of this prestigious role. As one of my clients once quipped: "I've told buddies of mine to bear in mind the additional 'costs' they will see in retirement. Between the car allowance and the expense account—it adds up!"

Loss of Status

We tend to be reluctant to admit that high status—as associated with prestige and wealth—is something we actively pursue. But humans are actually wired to seek status as a way of protecting their role in the community; so, it's more natural than we may realize.[9] Moreover, though a retired CEO may still have a great deal more status than the average person, they may experience subtle shifts in their community standing, access to decision-makers, and even ease of making a hard-to-get dinner reservation.

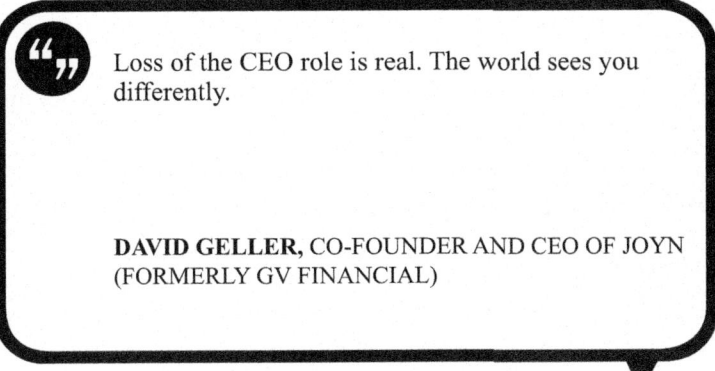

> Loss of the CEO role is real. The world sees you differently.
>
> **DAVID GELLER,** CO-FOUNDER AND CEO OF JOYN (FORMERLY GV FINANCIAL)

Many find this surprising and frustrating and, at times, demeaning. In multiple social circles, you will have gone effectively from being "top dog" to "just another suit," as echoed in the statement a client once shared:

>  The time I felt the most 'put out to pasture' was at a local Chamber of Commerce event where I had previously been President and actively sought out by many local businesses for my guidance and thoughts, and was now described as someone who 'used to run ABC company' and have the person politely shake my hand and quickly look to speak with someone more in the center of the active business community.
>
> RETIRED CEO OF INSURANCE COMPANY BASED IN THE SOUTHEAST

Lack of Purpose

One of the great values of our roles is that they clarify for us and for others what we are supposed to be doing—broadly, how we are expected to contribute to the world. A doctor takes care of patients, engages in medical research, or both; that is the purpose and responsibility that comes with that role, which gives meaning to the efforts of those in that occupation. This is powerful, because as humans our quality of life is enhanced when we have meaningful goals to pursue. Their presence gives direction and structure to the efforts we put forth, enabling us to feel like we matter or make a difference in the universe, as this quote from Betty Friedan's book *Fountain of Age* suggests:

> To be part of the community, to be part of something larger than oneself, to contribute somehow to the ongoing human enterprise, to pass on some legacy to the next generation, is, it seems, a burning need of vital age, different from the parenting of one's children yet just as essential to survival of the human species.[10]

When retirement leads to the loss of a central and all-consuming role and the person retiring has had little time or interest in developing other roles involving meaningful goals, their post-work life can seem directionless, or at least significantly diminished.

> While my passion for what I do now is strong, nothing can capture the special passion that I clearly had as family business CEO.
>
> **LANSE CRANE,** FORMER CEO OF CRANE & COMPANY

If, on the other hand, a retiring leader has a strong ability to develop new goals (or has long been pursuing outside interests), it is expected that they may look forward to retirement because they can envision meaningful ways to use their time and energy. As evidence, researchers have found that older adults who replace former meaningful goals and activities with new meaningful objectives and pursuits are less likely to experience depression.[11] In fact, in speaking with CEOs who have thrived in their transition to retirement, it's clear that they feel energized by the new challenges they are pursuing in areas where they have held longtime interest (but may have been unable to pursue fully while working) and where they are able to play a meaningful role.

David Juday, former CEO of test and measurement equipment company Ideal Industries, for example, told me how much he enjoys his diverse postwork roles: He has pursued woodworking, including making bowls for a church project; served on a bank's board of directors; mentored rising entrepreneurs; provided scholarships to undocumented and homeless children in the community; and supported the varied pursuits of his own family members.

As this example suggests, it isn't so much just doing something in retirement as much as doing things you find *challenging and meaningful*, as was clearly the case for David. Some CEOs with whom I spoke were pursuing big, time-consuming goals that may have rivaled those of their work lives, while others, like the former CEO client quoted below, were looking to make significant contributions while maintaining a life balanced with more leisure.

 One of the things I love about all my board work is that it is challenging and interesting, keeps me current on business issues and traveling some. But it also affords me the time to spend weeks on end on my boat with my wife, and allows me the time to pursue one-on-one activities of shared passion with each of my kids. It is such a gift to have the time and health to do all of these things.

RETIRED FAMILY BUSINESS LEADER, GLOBAL MANUFACTURER BASED IN NORTHEAST

Avoid the Identity Trap

As a first step in addressing the Identity Trap, evaluate the degree to which your work role defines your identity, using the questionnaire in Table 3.1 developed for this book. Note that the scoring guide for all tools and questionnaires in the book will be found in Appendix 3.

Rather than a scientific instrument, this questionnaire is meant as a simple thought exercise to help you reflect on the extent to which your work role is the dominant one in your life, which will help you understand how much of a loss you'll face as you transition away from that role. If you score on the lower end here, you likely have more "role complexity" than many business leaders and may not find the transition process that difficult. On the other hand, a high score suggests that you may want to invest extra energy in developing other interests or investing in other parts of your life so that you may feel that there are more parts to yourself, potentially reducing the associated sense of loss.

Wherever you score on the assessment, there follow several tips for avoiding the fallout related to loss of professional identity upon retirement. Ideally, you can put these into action well before your actual retirement begins.

Table 3.1: Centrality of Work Role

Please circle the answer to the right of each question that most closely reflects your response.

QUESTION	Score to attribute for each answer below:				
	1	2	3	4	5
For how many years have you been in your current role?	Less than 5 years	5 to 10 years	10 to 15 years	15 to 20 years	Over 20 years
How many hours a week do you work on average?	20 or less	20 to 40	40 to 55	56 to 70	Over 70
How hard would it be to come up with something to do if you were suddenly presented with a day free from any work responsibilities?	Very Easy	Easy	I'd figure something out	Hard	Very Hard
How often does your work or company come up in conversations when you are not at work?	Almost never	Rarely	About half the time	Pretty regularly	Always
You check and respond to phone call, email or texts from work in the evenings, on weekends & on vacation	Almost never	Rarely	About half the time	Pretty regularly	Always
How many substantive interests do you have outside of work to which you regularly commit time and energy?	More than 5	3 to 5	1 to 2	1	0
How many <u>good friends</u> do you have that have nothing to do with your work life?	More than 5	3 to 5	1 to 2	1	0
If you had to introduce yourself without referencing your work, how hard would it be to come up with a description of who you are?	Very Easy	Easy	I'd figure something out	Hard	Very Hard
TALLY YOUR SCORE (number of responses per column times the allocated score)	_x 1	_x 2	_x 3	_x 4	_x 5
FINAL SCORE = SUM: _____	=___ +	___ +	___ +	___ +	___

1. Recognize Over-Commitment to Your Professional Identity

Be aware of the extent to which you are committed to your professional role to the exclusion of the development of other meaningful roles and pursuits.

>  I was stunned at how much of my ego and persona became attached to the title, role, and business—just how much of an emotional sway the position had on me, despite my best efforts to 'guard my heart' against it.
>
> **DICK DEVOS,** FORMER PRESIDENT OF AMWAY

Of course, while working it can be difficult to find the bandwidth to engage in much else, especially early in your career, as you are focused on building your business and your leadership, while perhaps also contributing to raising a family. Even if you recognize such over-commitment, addressing it immediately may not always be practical. So, at the very least, find ways to enrich and broaden your *professional* roles where possible. For example, ensure your leadership gives you a chance to engage in both analytical work and mentorship (at the team or individual level).

Your mindset matters, too. Marilyn Carlson Nelson, former Chair and CEO of Carlson, talks below about how observing the identity struggles of other family business leaders, including within her business, helped her broaden her perspective.

My father, Curt Carlson, founded and propelled our company forward for 60 years. While I saw the value of the entrepreneur's passion, I could also see the organization's vulnerability when the leader's identity is nearly 100% tied to the role.

I became the CEO at age 59. I brought to the job several previous titles including securities analyst for Paine Webber, chair and board member of several corporate and non-profit organizations, the executive positions I had held within the family business as well as the all-important titles of wife and mother. When I accepted the role of CEO, I wrote myself a note that stated I would only stay on for 10 years in that role. I think because I saw this as a 'term in office,' I never defined myself by this role.

MARILYN CARLSON NELSON, FORMER CHAIR AND CEO OF CARLSON

2. Develop Other Interests

While it's important to have interests outside of work, as emphasized in this chapter, sometimes you can leverage the roles you play through work or family to facilitate minor extensions of your interests. For example, get involved in leadership for your industry trade association or serve on the board of your kids' school or a small local non-profit. Ideally, over time you can broaden your outreach to invest yourself in athletic interests, hobbies, or civic organizations that are fulfilling to you as a person.

It's important that the interests feel genuine to you. Former US President Jimmy Carter took on many post-work roles, from founding the Carter Center to advance human rights to volunteering with Habitat for Humanity—where he would go out on projects and simply cut siding alongside other volunteers. By all accounts, he embraced each new role, rather than comparing it to what he'd experienced as president.[12]

As an exercise related to your interests, take a few minutes to complete the worksheet in Table 3.2, to reflect on how and where your time is being invested today, and how those allocations are aligned—or misaligned—with your broader vision of yourself. The possible roles listed are not meant to be exhaustive, and there are a few blank spaces at the bottom if there are others you'd like to add. How you fill it out should provide clues for the interests you'd like to indulge more fully.

Table 3.2: Role Allocation

Please use the first column to allocate how you spend your time today, the second column to allocate how you would LIKE to be spending your time, and the third to note some obstacles you anticipate in moving towards that desired state.

ROLE	Percentage of your waking time (today)	Percentage of your waking time (desired allocation)	Obstacles in moving towards that desired state
Primary Work Role (Job)			
Other Business or Professional Roles (Board, mentor, side ventures, trade assoc., etc.)			
Spouse			
Other Family Relationships (time with children, extended family…)			
Friends			
Engaging with Faith or Spirituality			
Volunteer			
Pursuing meaningful hobby, fitness, or sport			
Other:			
Other:			
TOTAL	100%	100%	

3. Take Planning Seriously

Give real time and thought to how you will fill your days when you are no longer leading the business. "Travel and golf" is not a sufficient answer, unless you are a passionate golfer and have many friends with whom you can share this interest and who can push you to keep growing your skills, or are determined to see more of the world and have the means to do so and multiple people with whom you would enjoy traveling. Sit down and think through your daily routine, asking yourself serious questions. What goals will you pursue? How will you pursue them? Who will it involve? Where will you go—how often? How will you feel you are making meaningful impact and leveraging your knowledge and contacts productively? As Lanse Crane, former CEO of

Crane & Company, recalled, "I knew there are other lives out there." Think about which of those other lives you most want to pursue in retirement.

4. Understand—and Plan—for What You'll Lose

As you plan your transition out of leadership, take stock of all the perks and benefits that come with your current role and consider which you need to replace. Bear in mind that this can impact your personal income—for example, if the company has paid your club membership to date, will this continue or do you need to budget for this expense? More challenging for many is losing the administrative support on which they have come to rely. Take honest stock of the personal (not related to business leadership) work your administrative team supports today, and think through how you will get these tasks done in future. Do you need to hire a part-time administrative assistant? Where will you house the files you need to access for your board or other professionally related roles?

5. Formalize Your Role

Give yourself a post-work title. That may sound funny or contrived, but it helps to think through how you want to describe what it is you do now that you are not going to be the CEO or leader of the enterprise. You can make this lighthearted if that is in keeping with your personal style: "Retiree in Training" or "Designated Trouble-maker" may go on your business card. I have seen many family leaders modify their business card to say "Shareholder"; a simple adjustment like that can maintain elegantly your affiliation with your family's business.

6. Practice Your Pitch

Just as you practiced for countless presentations and speeches as CEO, it can be helpful to practice describing what you do in your post-work life. Hopefully, you will have started to envision a role or series of roles for yourself now that you have new bandwidth to deploy.

Now think through how you would articulate this to an old friend at a reunion or to a person you meet at a conference. Even a short description can do the job: "I currently divide my time between board service for a couple enterprises and an education task force for our mayor, along with spending quality time with my family and fly fishing whenever I can."

> 'I am CEO of Robbie' is what I told people for many years. I may get to a place where I say 'I am a teacher' or 'I am a full-time volunteer philanthropic guy'.
>
> **IRV ROBINSON,** CO-FOUNDER AND FORMER CEO OF ROBBIE FANTASTIC FLEXIBLES

Notes

1. William Bridges, *Transitions: Making Sense of Life's Changes* (Da Capo Press, Cambridge, 2004), p. 116.
2. Stephen Covey, *The Seven Habits of Highly Effective People: Powerful Lessons in Personal Change* (Simon & Schuster, New York, 1989).
3. As reported by Lydia Saad, "The "40-Hour" Work Week is Actually Longer—by 7 Hours," *Gallup.com*, August 29, 2014, http://www.gallup.com/poll/175286/hour-workweek-actually-longer-seven-hours.aspx (accessed January 27, 2016).
4. For an academic perspective on this issue, see Peter J. Burke and Donald C. Reitzes, "An Identity Theory Approach to Commitment," *Social Psychology Quarterly*, September 1991, 54(3), pp. 239–251.
5. S. Gee and J. Baillie, "Happily Ever After? An Exploration of Retirement Expectations," *Educational Gerontology*, 1999, 25, pp. 109–128.
6. See, for example, Nancy Schlossberg, *Revitalizing Retirement: Reshaping your Identity, Relationships, and Purpose* (American Psychological Association, Washington, DC, 2009).
7. Max Nisen, "Top CEOs Work Crazy Hours Even on Normal Days," *Business Insider*, April 4, 2013, http://www.businessinsider.com/top-ceo-schedules-2013-4 (accessed January 27, 2016).
8. For more on this transition-related challenge, see William Bridges and Susan Bridges, *Managing Transitions* (Da Capo, Philadelphia, 2009).
9. See, for example, David Rock, "SCARF: A Brain-based Model for Collaborating with and Influencing Others," *NeuroLeadership Journal*, 2008, 1, 1–9.
10. Betty Friedan, *Fountain of Age* (Simon & Schuster, New York, 1993, p. 613).
11. Y. Benyamini and J. Lomranz, "The Relationship of Activity Restriction and Replacement with Depressive Symptoms Among Older Adults," *Psychology and Aging*, 2004, 19, pp. 362–366.
12. See for example Carter-related anecdotes in Peter Buffett, *Life Is What You Make It*, Three Rivers Press, New York, 2010.

4

How Ready Are You for Change?

Phil Clemens, former CEO of the Clemens Family Corporation, told me the story of another family business leader, a founder who had begun transitioning ownership of his business to his adult children—all held management roles with the firm—some years ago. When the children hinted that he could start thinking about retirement, the founder became livid. He fired his children and repurchased all the shares he'd granted them. Now, years later, the founder's health is failing but he is unwilling to sell the business to management or an outside buyer, in part because he has no plan for retirement: he is unsure what he would do day to day. Not surprisingly, his relationships with his children are strained, given past dynamics, so it's also unclear how much contact he would have with them going forward.

This cautionary tale relates well to the idea of the identity trap we discussed in Chapter 3, or how family business leaders as a group struggle with their transition to post-work life because their professional role takes up too much of their identity. Phil's acquaintance had clearly staked too much of his identity in the business he'd founded, with wide-reaching negative consequences.

The story also illustrates the idea that the *individual* leader is at the center of the personal continuity readiness model we are using here (as depicted in Fig. 4.1), because each person experiences differently the changes and challenges related to the transition away from work. Specifically, a person's internal wiring around comfort with change, optimism, need to be in charge, and more will impact their experience of this transition and will likely affect how others experience these changes as well, helping to determine how much difficulty the whole *system* will face related to the transition. Further, a retiring leader's health situation can also be a powerful driver of what is possible (and not possible), and

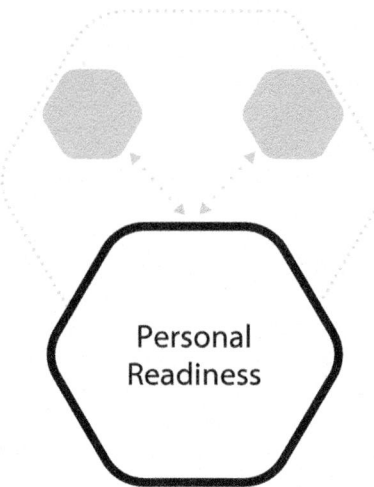

Fig. 4.1 Personal readiness

how the process plays itself out. These factors will interact with your experience to influence your comfort with the transition to post-work life and how well that transition goes, in the short and longer term, for the entire system.

This chapter considers multiple aspects of internal readiness, including those common to most anyone making the transition and those that will vary significantly from leader to leader.

Change Is Hard

"[I]f heart doctors tell their seriously at-risk heart patients they will literally *die* if they do not make changes to their personal lives—diet, exercise, smoking—*still* only one in seven is actually able to make the changes."[1] That sad research-based truth illustrates just how hard change is. Even when people know that maintaining the status quo will be life threatening, they find the process of change intimidating and uncomfortable and often resist it altogether. A part of the problem is that people struggle to handle the uncertainty of what things will be like after a change, experiencing real fear or stress about that ambiguity.

At the same time, most of us understand that growth cannot happen without change, as much as we may wish that weren't the case. For example, business leaders talk about "creative destruction"—a term coined by Joseph Schumpter in the 1940s[2]—as part of the innovation and improvement they seek to bring to the market, whether introducing new technology or disrupting an entire industry, as Uber and Airbnb have done for the transportation and lodging markets, respectively. Most of us have had the experience of being out of our depths in a new role, having to learn and change, and becoming more capable through those hard efforts, growing consequently into better leaders or professionals.

There's no doubt some of us innately accept and adapt to change more easily than others. Your ability to navigate all the changes that come with the transition to retirement will definitely have a bearing on how the process plays out. As retirement is a later-life phenomenon, the idea that we become more resistant to change as we age will also be relevant. At the same time, features of your specific situation may impact your comfort with the changes—especially when objectively you have more or less control over outcomes.

In the next sections, we will consider how health and well-being, the ability to adjust life goals, and temperament or personality influence your internal readiness to take on the changes needed to transition successfully out of your business leadership role.

Before we move into the sections that follow, assess your general readiness for change using this simplified questionnaire (Table 4.1).[3]

Table 4.1: General Readiness for Change

Circle the number beside each statement that reflects how accurately the statement describes you in general. Please don't overthink your responses – go with your clearest impression.

Not Like Me	A little like me	A lot like me	Exactly Like Me
1	2	3	4

1. I prefer the familiar to the unknown	1	2	3	4
2. I get impatient when there are no clear answers	1	2	3	4
3. I am inclined to establish routines and stay with them	1	2	3	4
4. When something important doesn't work out, it takes me time to adjust	1	2	3	4
5. I get frustrated when I can't get a grip on something	1	2	3	4
6. I prefer staying with the tried and true approach to things	1	2	3	4
7. I find it hard to give up on something, even if it isn't working out	1	2	3	4
8. I can't stand to leave things unfinished	1	2	3	4

SCORING Add up all the numbers you circled, for a TOTAL: _____

Turn to Appendix 3 for a simple "measure" of your readiness to change based on this assessment. Not surprisingly, if you typically find change difficult, you can expect the transition process to be harder for you than for most others. That's not to say you should "let yourself off the hook" of doing the hard work of the transition but that you should have some empathy for yourself and look for ways to gain support during the change, whether that be a group of peers who are facing similar challenges or a coach or advisor to help you through the process. You may also want to ask your family and board of directors to hold you accountable for making progress toward the transition. Later sections of this chapter offer additional tips.

> I think what drove me most of my career was a fear of failure, and I have met a *lot* of CEOs who will 'fess up' to the same thing.
>
> **JACK HERSCHEND,** FORMER CEO OF HERSCHEND ENTERTAINMENT

Temperament

Personality and temperament play a large role in your response to change. Your temperament is your innate wiring, or the aspects of your personality or bearing with which you came into the world, as opposed to characteristics you may have learned over time. The classic example is the dimension of introversion and extroversion. Do you get more energy from quiet and reflective time on your own or from social interaction and idea-sharing with others? These dimensions are not black and white, as no one is 100% introverted or extroverted. While we can lean more toward one pole in a given situation, most of us have a general preference for one end of the spectrum or the other, and this natural tendency has a pronounced effect on our choices, thoughts, and behavior.

In the context of a transition out of leadership, two specific personality characteristics that may make the shift easier for some leaders than others are openness to experience and need for control.

Openness to Experience

Like introversion-extroversion, openness to experience is known as one of the "Big Five" personality traits, or the five core dimensions that characterize personality in a way that helps us predict how an individual might respond in a given situation.[4] Within this framework, those who have a higher measure of openness to experience tend to think flexibly and are more receptive to new ideas than do those who are less open. They may be more willing to accept the idea that a fully lived life means that there will be the occasional mess-up or misstep along the way.[5] Individuals described as having a lower openness to experience tend to prefer the status quo,[6] and thus might be expected to have more difficulty with change, including the transition to retirement.

Assess your level of openness to experience using the questionnaire labeled Table 4.2, which has been adapted from academic tools.[7] Note the extent to

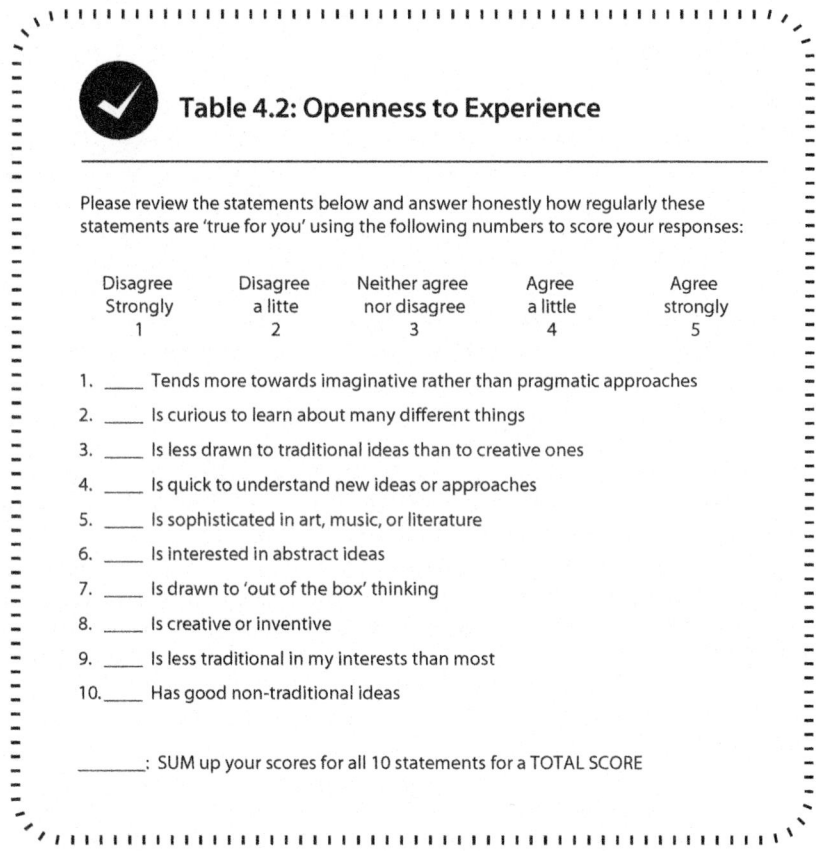

Table 4.2: Openness to Experience

Please review the statements below and answer honestly how regularly these statements are 'true for you' using the following numbers to score your responses:

Disagree Strongly	Disagree a litte	Neither agree nor disagree	Agree a little	Agree strongly
1	2	3	4	5

1. ____ Tends more towards imaginative rather than pragmatic approaches
2. ____ Is curious to learn about many different things
3. ____ Is less drawn to traditional ideas than to creative ones
4. ____ Is quick to understand new ideas or approaches
5. ____ Is sophisticated in art, music, or literature
6. ____ Is interested in abstract ideas
7. ____ Is drawn to 'out of the box' thinking
8. ____ Is creative or inventive
9. ____ Is less traditional in my interests than most
10. ____ Has good non-traditional ideas

_____: SUM up your scores for all 10 statements for a TOTAL SCORE

which you agree with the set of statements. As with other tools here, try to answer quickly and not over-think your response, the scoring key is found in Appendix 3 (Scoring Guide 4.2):

One interesting aspect of openness to experience is that entrepreneurs tend to score higher on this trait than managers,[8] yet we find family business founders—entrepreneurs, by definition—to be among the CEOs who struggle the most with the transition out of their leadership role. It may be that the innovative and curious mind that comes with openness to experience helps entrepreneurs take the right risks to get a business started, yet it is also possible that the extent to which that business becomes central to their identity (see Chapter 3 for more on this identity trap) prevents these entrepreneurs from having the same flexibility around evolving their role at a later stage in life.

While a person with higher openness to experience will generally be more receptive to new ideas and experiences than another who scores low on this dimension, other factors also play a role. For example, as we age, we all tend to get a little more set in our ways, so our openness to experience may diminish; and this may also help explain why the once-young entrepreneurs formerly more open to experience then struggle with the idea of experiences other than running their business as they move toward retirement age. In addition, humans are "loss averse", meaning we react more strongly to losses than to the equivalent gains—for example, people feel more negatively about losing $20 than they feel positively about finding $20, even though the amount is the same.[9] This suggests that the losses inherent to a transition from the CEO role feel far more costly and difficult than the benefits you may anticipate from the associated gains, such as freedom to pursue new opportunities.

If you find you are on the lower end of openness to experience scale (given your score on the assessment in Table 4.2 and other evidence), it may be helpful for you to reflect on ways you can continue to contribute or engage that feel similar to the roles you have held in the past. That is, you may be happier pursuing opportunities within your industry's trade association, mentoring other professionals, serving on boards of businesses—as opposed to exploring more divergent paths such as writing a book, taking on a civic project, or pursuing classes.

Need for Control

Need for control is another personality characteristic that may help us understand why the transition from the CEO role is so difficult for many business leaders. In working with families grappling with this transition, I often hear

CEOs indicate that they are moving toward retirement by spending more time at their vacation home or generally away from the office; yet, they still engage in controlling behavior by calling the office regularly to provide clear direction for management, demanding constant and detailed updates on business matters, and further actions which others may experience as intrusive. Leaders who are even quite ill will seek reassurance that their control mechanisms remain firmly in place, as evidenced in this classic story of an old man on his deathbed:

> As he lay there with his eyes closed, his wife whispered to him, naming every member of the family who was there to wish him shalom, "And who," he suddenly asked, sitting up abruptly, "who is minding the store?"[10]

It's reasonable to conjecture that individuals who go out and start businesses may do so in part because they are ambitious and want to control their own destiny. This implies, in turn, that entrepreneurs may have a higher need for control than those who are not business-builders, and that a transition that leaves them in a position of diminished power and control may make them quite uncomfortable. In fact, many CEOs get to their position because they are achievement-driven individuals, or "Type A" people. While no one relishes the experience of loss of control and the fear of losing control is associated with aging in general, Type A individuals in particular may resist retirement—as a way to fend off the anxiety and helplessness they associate with this later phase of life.[11]

One pattern among my interviewees is that success with navigating the transition from leadership is associated with the departing CEOs' approach to power and control. While most of these individuals were unambiguously powerful leaders who had transformed their enterprises in meaningful ways over decades, many saw their role as akin to that of *servant leader and steward*. In some cases, this was an evolution. That is, they had a period earlier in their leadership where they had to be more controlling to bring about certain difficult changes for the enterprise, but they moved consciously toward a more inclusive style of leadership once they had won those early battles.

Phil Clemens speaks to the pros and cons of servant leadership:

"You get a lot of CEOs who are pride-driven; but then there are those who are humble servant leaders. It's about not trying to make yourself more than you are. In fact, the lower role you take, the higher people will place you. But servant leaders have a problem that they don't want recognition. You do need to receive recognition and receive it graciously—don't rob people of their joy of giving or showing you appreciation."

It may be that leaders who are—or learn to be—less directive and accept that they cannot control everything, may be able to leverage this acceptance-related skill in their transition to a next phase. For example, if they have learned that the business functions well without them making every key decision, it may be easier to walk away with confidence.

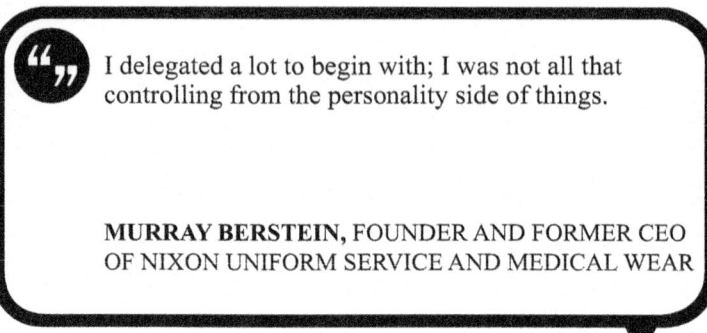

> I delegated a lot to begin with; I was not all that controlling from the personality side of things.
>
> **MURRAY BERSTEIN,** FOUNDER AND FORMER CEO OF NIXON UNIFORM SERVICE AND MEDICAL WEAR

But it's also possible that an individual's internal need for control may create significant distortions in how they see the business functioning. For instance, an individual with a strong need for control could convince him- or herself that the management team just isn't ready for their departure, that decisions where they (the CEO) are less engaged inevitably go awry, that key customers would not agree to work with anyone else, and so on. Many of my interviewees spoke of observing leaders well past their prime, including their own family members, who stayed in their roles too long, believing they were still having a positive impact. As one interviewee said of his parent, the former top executive: "She was the only one who didn't realize it was time for her to go."

In many cases, personality traits can interact with the business situation in a cyclical way. For example, many overly directive leaders get into a cycle such that their need for control motivates them to shape the enterprise carefully to their vision, and subsequently to have more opportunities to lead more things, which makes it even more difficult for them to step away at the logical end of their tenure. By contrast, servant leaders tend to see their role in the context of the *team* and thus feel less need for control, which creates a more virtuous cycle. They are more likely to work to empower others, which enables them to develop successors more effectively, which ultimately helps them accept their "replace-ability" and transition out of the leadership role.

In addition, more servant-oriented leaders develop skills in mentoring others, which may yield them more opportunities for their own post-work engagement and contribution. Many of the CEO interviewees spoke of how much they have enjoyed mentoring other business and civic leaders since leaving their leadership role. While mentoring is among the classic "generativity" activities that psychologist Erik Erikson suggests are critical tasks of later life,[12] it may not come naturally to everyone but is probably a skill that *anyone* can improve.

As these aspects of your personality style may help you appreciate how the transition process may be more or less difficult for you, rate yourself on your own need to be in charge or in control using the scale in Table 4.3,[13] rate yourself on servant-leadership qualities using the scale in Table 4.4. As with any tool like this, being honest with yourself will provide you with more actionable insights.

As with the other assessments in this book, the scoring guides are found in Appendix 3. Anecdotally, most of the leaders I interviewed, especially those thriving in post-work life, demonstrated a tendency toward servant leadership. We could guess that this style might lead to greater ease with transition, because those who demonstrate it tend to define success in terms of the development and achievements of others. This means that such leaders would take

---

✓ Table 4.3: Desire for Control

Please review the statements below and answer honestly how regularly these statements are 'true for you' using the following numbers to score your responses:

Never	Seldom	Sometimes	Frequently	Always
1	2	3	4	5

1. ____ I enjoy being able to influence the actions of others.
2. ____ I enjoy having control over my own destiny.
3. ____ My ideas are good and I try to persuade other people to accept them.
4. ____ I only share information with others when I feel they are ready to hear it.
5. ____ I try to avoid situations where someone else tries to tell me what to do.
6. ____ I like to be in charge of things.
7. ____ I am concerned about my reputation.
8. ____ I try to do better than other people on things that I do.

_____: SUM up your scores for all 8 statements for a TOTAL SCORE

Table 4.4: Servant Leadership Style

In thinking about how you typically approach your work responsibilities, please indicate your level of agreement or disagreement with the following statements. Please answer the questions as honestly as possible – considering how others might perceive you as a 'gut check'.

	Disagree strongly 1	Disagree a litte 2	Agree a little 3	Agree strongly 4

I support others in their efforts to do their best work	1	2	3	4
Good bosses make all employees feel important	1	2	3	4
I try to communicate a welcoming attitude to everyone I meet	1	2	3	4
I constantly look for ways to serve others	1	2	3	4
I almost always see the positive potential in others	1	2	3	4
I work hard to try to enrich the lives of those who are less fortunate than me	1	2	3	4
I work to create an environment where each person feels understood	1	2	3	4
My first priority in life is to serve	1	2	3	4
I encourage others to provide me with constructive criticism of my performance so I can improve	1	2	3	4
I get immense pleasure from seeing others grow & develop	1	2	3	4

Add up all the numbers you circled to tally a TOTAL SCORE: _____

great pride in building a team that can carry on well without them. A more "command-and-control" leader, in contrast, might find the transition more difficult, as they tend to base fulfillment more on a sense of their own efforts and achievement.

In general, though, be careful not to think of personality types as either "good" or "bad" in this context. It's more the case that some characteristics are better-suited to some situations than others. A high need for control or a directive leadership style, for example, may fit better with some specific community, volunteer, or entrepreneurial roles or activities than others. Do your best to know—and accept—yourself and to use that knowledge to inform your planning for this process, develop some empathy for yourself, and shape your post-work activities, so that these lead to maximum fulfillment.

Goal Flexibility

Goals matter. The significance we attribute to having control in a given situation will certainly be affected by the importance of that situation to our lives, identity, and sense of purpose—or the goals we associate with that domain of life. As has been discussed throughout the book, our sense of having a meaningful purpose and feeling relevant or needed is critically important to our well-being. Individuals pursuing personally meaningful goals report greater emotional well-being, lower depression, lower perceived stress, and greater physical health than those who pursue less meaningful goals.[14] In fact, one of the central challenges of aging is that it may come with the loss of meaningful roles and a resulting broad sense of loss of purpose and loss of value, as discussed in depth in Chapter 3.

Goal Disengagement and Reengagement

While we all need purpose, it is both normal and appropriate for our roles and goals to evolve over the course of our lives. In fact, it is often best to abandon a goal if it is leading mostly to failure and frustration—and this is a situation which some of us can identify and adjust to more easily than others. The term used to describe this process is *goal disengagement*, defined as the reduction of effort and psychological commitment directed at a goal that a person should logically stop pursuing to preserve their well-being.[15] For example, one might be letting go of the goal of giving birth to a child when you are a woman well past child-bearing age. If a person can reduce the importance of this goal in their mind, letting go becomes less painful.

>  In many ways, I was delighted to step aside – really had no interest in going to a bunch of meetings or continuing the road warrior life. That part of it was pretty easy to walk away from. I attend our family meetings and make a contribution if I can – but the idea is to pass the baton on to the next generation.
>
> The reality is that institutional knowledge has a shelf-life, times change. Whatever you might have done – the early jobs you had often don't exist anymore – as a result, you have a whole background of useless knowledge to some degree.
> If we are not current, we are not useful.
>
> **FRANK SCHURZ**, FORMER CEO OF SCHURZ COMMUNICATION

Putting this in the context of a CEO who might best be served by letting go of the goal of continuing to lead his or her business, we would expect those who can convince themselves that holding the leadership post is no longer in their best interest (too much travel and stress, not enough time to pursue other interests) will have an easier time de-committing from their role at the business's helm. Moreover, my own research suggests that strong goal disengagement capability does link to more positive expectations for retirement among business leaders.[16]

Of course, when it comes to family business leadership, making this change by disengaging from work-related goals can be far trickier in practice than in theory. For instance, it is often the case that the CEO is not experiencing any failure or frustration in their role, and may even be thriving, having the time of their lives. Even so, it might still be to the long-term benefit of the family, organization, and broader systems that this leader transition out. In this reality for many family firms, we are asking someone to abandon a goal (leading their business) that is continuing to provide much fulfillment. This is clearly more difficult than walking away from a goal associated mostly with frustration and failure.

> There will be a time where I go through some 'withdrawal' pains - you know, I am in the middle of the action, I get to make a difference, I get to create - so what I will try to do is go to places where I can duplicate that… I am hopeful that I will have enough opportunities that I can do some of the same things I have been able to do here & do them in some other places. I don't know if anything else will be as meaningful - but I am pretty hopeful about it.
>
> **IRV ROBINSON,** TALKING ABOUT HIS HOPES AND CONCERNS FOR HIS TRANSITION FROM LEADING ROBBIE FANTASTIC FLEXIBLES, A COMPANY HE FOUNDED.

In this context, your ability to develop new meaningful goals is particularly important. In psychology, this concept is called *reengagement*, defined as the ability to identify, commit to, and pursue alternative meaningful goals after having to abandon a previously valued goal (such as business leadership).[17] The expectation is that if a CEO has—or can develop—a number of non-work-related goals toward which to direct their passion and energy, this helps ease the loss of the leadership role upon retirement, and continues to give their life purpose and meaning. In the interviews for this book, time and again I was impressed by the power that new or alternative goals had to make this transition successful on paper, and joyful in practice.

One of the benefits of reengagement is that it typically leads to growth and development, which are important to our sense of thriving, no matter our age. As Henry Ford said, "Anyone who stops learning is old, whether at twenty or eighty. Anyone who keeps learning stays young."[18] Walking away from a work role that has led to much success and fulfillment is of course daunting, but I heard several CEOs talk about the newfound energy they accessed in tackling new challenges and passionate pursuits.

Now that we've discussed the concepts of goal disengagement/reengagement, assess yourself on these measures using the questionnaire in Table 4.5, and then review the scoring key in Appendix 3 after you have completed this exercise.[19]

Individuals who have a harder time disengaging will naturally have more difficulty leaving their leadership role. If you struggle in this area, anticipate the challenge you may face and seek support among your family, board, and outside advisors in approaching the transition. Similarly, if you have a hard time with reengagement, you may need to be quite proactive here, and invest

Table 4.5: Capacity for Disengagement and Reengagement

During their lives people cannot always attain what they want and are sometimes forced to stop pursuing the goals they have set. How do you usually react when this happens to you?

Please indicate the extent to which you agree or disagree with each of the following statements, as it usually applies to you.

Disagree Strongly	Disagree a litte	Neither agree nor disagree	Agree a little	Agree strongly
1	2	3	4	5

If I have to stop pursuing an important goal in my life:

I stay committed to the goal for a long time; I can't let it go	1 2 3 4 5
It's difficult for me to stop thinking about the goal	1 2 3 4 5
I find it difficult to reduce my desire to achieve the goal	1 2 3 4 5
It's hard for me to reduce my effort towards the goal	1 2 3 4 5

SUM up above scores for a total on **Disengagement:** _____

I seek other meaningful goals	1 2 3 4 5
I convince myself that I have other meaningful goals to pursue	1 2 3 4 5
I start working on other new goals	1 2 3 4 5
I think about other new goals to pursue	1 2 3 4 5
I tell myself that I have a number of other new goals to draw upon	1 2 3 4 5
I put effort toward other meaningful goals	1 2 3 4 5

SUM up above scores for a total on **Reengagement:** _____

more time exploring other pursuits to see which might capture your interest and help you discover a path to ongoing life fulfillment and purpose past your day-to-day leadership of the enterprise.

Goal Shifts Are Never Easy

While this book's aim is to share success stories to provide inspiration and ideas for those considering their own leadership exit, it is important to recognize that even for those who have found satisfaction in retirement, the process to get there is not without challenges. As William Bridges suggests in his book *Transitions*, "Even though the external 'new beginning' may happen very quickly … the internal re-identification and re-engagement always occur more slowly."[20] In line with this, my interviews showed that for some former leaders, the process of reengaging took time, and for many, finding an adequate way of identifying and describing their newly diverse roles—to themselves and others—remains a struggle. As my mother, a retired leader herself, described to me recently:

> "Though I am now doing a great many things that I enjoy, from volunteering as a museum docent, leading an initiative at my alma mater, spending more time with family and friends, spearheading an arts funding effort, traveling, and learning Spanish, it took some time to develop this portfolio of activities, and I still sometimes struggle to answer that old chestnut: 'What do you do?'"

The Indignities of Aging ("*Growing Old Is Not for Sissies*")

Retirement is associated with aging, and the aging process includes many features that make the transition to post-work life even more challenging. Let's consider some of the most influential factors.

Health Crises

In addition to the challenges and learning curve anyone experiences with new opportunities, aging may also bring unwanted changes in physical health that can impact a CEO's transition by making new opportunities that much harder to take on. While measures to assess physical health and vitality are outside the scope of this book, the experience of serious health obstacles often precipitate a

CEO's exit from leadership, and may well curtail the options open to him or her in retirement. In many ways, this is particularly cruel because individuals who are forced into retirement by medical conditions may have done the least amount of planning and could benefit the most emotionally from finding purposeful ways to engage with life and reclaim some sense of mastery and control.

My fellow consultants and I often stress to family business clients that continuity planning should be a *process* and not an event, because we have seen too many cases where no planning was done and a health crisis suddenly puts an entire business enterprise at risk, as in the example that follows:

> **Health Crisis Leads to Forced Sale**
>
> *Joe was a charismatic leader who had taken his father's small construction business and built it into a significant regional player while adding a large commercial real estate portfolio to the family's holdings. Though he had recruited strong talent to his financial and operations teams, he was very much a hub-and-spoke leader, with all decisions going through him—until he suffered a massive, debilitating stroke at his desk in his early 70s. While Joe's son and daughter were intelligent and had decades of experience with the business, they were ill-prepared to address all the decisions that came on the heels of this crisis. Their father had not kept them current on many key deals, and they didn't even know the details of all the bank accounts in the enterprise's name. As their mother had died several years earlier, much of their father's care fell on their shoulders. So, they were trying to manage the business while handling a series of complex medical decisions for which neither was ready. The resulting disorientation and power vacuum at the company led to tension and discord among the managers, some of whom were vying for authority and all of whom were worried about the business's ability to weather the storm. Creditors also became nervous. Several months after Joe's stroke, when a substantial line of credit was not renewed, his children were forced to sell the operating business for well below its value.*

There are too many stories like that one. Countless family businesses are at risk daily because their leaders are not willing to contemplate their mortality, nor start to share key information with decision-makers who will have to pick up the pieces when a health crisis occurs. Of course, it is worth remembering that while leaders may be more likely to fall gravely ill or die suddenly later in life, *all* businesses need a crisis plan, as the unexpected can strike leaders at any age. Planning for a crisis does not make it more likely you will experience a crisis, BUT it makes it FAR more likely that the organization can weather that storm.

But let's put aside the idea of a permanently impairing health condition for now. The harsh truth is that "growing old isn't for sissies," as my mother likes to say. Many, if not most, of us will confront our retirement years with at least minor physical limitations or reduced energy. Even if we are blessed with great genes and sustain strong health well into old age, eventually we will slow down and need to find ways to stay engaged and contribute. In light of this, thinking creatively about post-leadership opportunities for engagement may be particularly important for leaders whose health is in decline, even if it's a slow decline. Research suggests individuals facing significant existential threats (such as a health situation that may limit mobility or energy level) do better if they are able to reengage in fulfilling pursuits.[21]

This presents a challenge for retiring CEOs, because if they have a health situation that limits physical or mental functioning, it may be harder to find ways to contribute to society at a level that seems meaningful for them. The result of this is that finding a solution will require thinking creatively about <u>all</u> the ways you can contribute (rather than dwelling on the limitations, or paths no longer available) and putting a concerted effort into developing fulfilling post-work opportunities, using the resources still available to you. I provide some starter ideas in the "Staying Engaged Despite Health Limitations" box in Table 4.6.

Table 4.6: Staying Engaged Despite Health Limitations

- Serve on board of nonprofit organization
- Volunteer with disadvantaged groups (such as reading to children)
- Lead a fundraising effort for major non-profit or political campaign
- Speak to school or university groups about business or other
- Teach or mentor aspiring entrepreneurs or business leaders
- Speak to other family businesses about their business or governance challenges
- Go into public office, whether at the local, state, or national level
- Write a book on business, family history, or any topic on which you have deep knowledge

Ageism

Beyond a health crisis that may be an objectively limiting factor, many retired leaders also encounter ageism when they seek to take on new roles, finding that decision-makers assume they have limited energy or capability, given their age. Our culture puts a particular premium on youth and vitality, sometimes to the detriment of wisdom and calm—which may provide a valuable balance or perspective in many situations. As Gloria Steinem put it: "We've allowed a youth-centered culture to leave us so estranged from our future selves that, when asked about the years beyond fifty, sixty, or seventy ... many people can see only a blank screen, or one on which they project disease and dependency."[22]

One domain where ageism may be a challenge is boards of directors. Having conducted many director searches for family businesses, I appreciate the value of term limits to enable a board to bring in fresh perspectives and new ideas. However, when those limits are dictated by age, as they often are, the unintended consequence may be that individuals with tremendous experience and knowledge—along with time, patience, and energy—to serve as excellent directors are passed over because the board has an explicit age limit or there is a presumption that an older person (and especially a retired person) may be unable to keep pace or to really contribute to handling tomorrow's challenges.

This can be a difficult issue to overcome, as decision-makers will not always admit to their bias and may even be unaware of their discriminatory behavior in the first place. Ensuring your circle of professional and personal connections has age diversity can be a good counterbalance to this. If you engage regularly with younger professionals and listen with open ears to the wisdom of their perspective and experience, you will remain "in the know" and, as such, project and offer ongoing relevance and credibility.

Another way to stay current is by attending industry events and reading trade publications and newspapers. Indeed, I find many retired CEOs to be incredibly knowledgeable about the newest technologies and industry or business trends, in part because they have more time to read and stay current, and in part because those who make this transition to post-work life successfully are committed to lifelong learning and thus seek exposure to new ideas and opportunities that they can connect with their past experience—joining the dots in ways that are powerful and interesting.

I myself am only in my late 40s, but I'm struck even now at how the wisdom I have gained over the years informs my thinking and perspective on so many challenges—giving me a more balanced view, and truly helping me to find joy and satisfaction, even in the face of adversity. While there is a lot about youth to savor and appreciate, it is nonetheless incredible what a few gray hairs can provide in terms of a wider view. And being older honestly makes things more fun! Taking this lesson to heart can go a long way to smoothing your transition.

Loss of Relationships

One of the hardest parts of later life is that you start to lose peers to illness and old age. While we will address the cost of these losses to your support systems more fully in Chapter 5's discussion of family systems, bear in mind that grieving the death of family members, close friends, and other peers will also have a bearing on your internal well-being. The loss of a spouse or a sibling is both a powerful reminder of our own mortality and may lead naturally to a greater experience of isolation and loneliness. Some individuals may even suffer from clinical depression for a time after the death of a close family member. This profound emotional toll will impact your perceptions and mood, which will certainly color any planning or efforts around leadership transition.

As with most things, the impact of such losses can vary by individual. In some cases that I've observed, the death of a sibling or close friend prompts a CEO to reconsider their current situation and move more quickly toward retirement to pursue other passions, lest they lose the opportunity. Yet in other, similar situations I have seen a CEO cling more strongly to their leadership role, either unwilling to acknowledge their own mortality *or* so convinced they will be bored and lonely if they were to retire now that their brother/spouse/friend has died, that they become more entrenched and unwilling to pursue new paths.

How to Improve Your Personal Readiness

Here are some effective ways to enhance your personal readiness for the transition, built on the ideas in this chapter. It's best to work on these well before you actually make the transition into retirement, so you will be primed to make the most of it.

Push Yourself to Try New Things If you don't have interests beyond work, there will be very little to look forward to after your professional role ends. Even those with several well-developed interests can try new things, whether related to fitness, arts, culture, community/volunteering, travel, or other areas. Worst case, you'll find you don't want to pursue that particular interest. Best case, you'll discover something to help keep you occupied and engaged well into later life.

Know Your Need for Control and Find Arenas in Which to Use It You need to be honest with yourself about how comfortable you are relinquishing control. If the idea of having very little to direct post-retirement makes you feel like you will not be a full contributor, look for opportunities to take on some new leadership roles, whether through board membership, leadership of a volunteer organization, getting engaged in local government, or something similar. Ideally, it will be in an area that is meaningful to you, beyond just the potential for asserting some control.

Become a Mentor Mentorship is an excellent way to share your wisdom, stay plugged in, and keep young. Many of my interviewees shared how much they have enjoyed contributing meaningfully to the growth of an individual (or several!) and the organizations where that person is involved, as a mentor. In addition, investing in these ties strengthens your personal network, keeps you current, and protects you from isolation.

Network and Invest in New Relationships It's important to spend time making connections with people outside your traditional circles. You will be surprised by the opportunities this can generate, as well as the broader ideas you will be able to develop as you connect your knowledge and experience with new people.

Plan Your Path Toward Meaningful Roles Think hard about the ways that work brings you joy and fulfillment, in as broad terms as you can (such as moving projects forward, leading a team, and so on), and then find ways to continue such activities in a non-work role. This will leverage your strengths, enable you to contribute in new arenas, and provide you with more satisfaction through reengagement.

Get Involved Early It's a lot easier to continue a role in an outside-of-work organization after retirement than to find and start such a role at that point. So, it's best to take on such roles early in your career or to at least engage in active networking so that there are a wide range of decision-makers in your community who know you not just by reputation but through direct contact. This will yield more opportunity and also help you overcome ageism, as gatekeepers will be assured of your ability to contribute, having seen it firsthand.

Invest in Your Health This should go without saying, but it's important to state all the same: Take care of your health, so that you have the vitality and ability to pursue all the opportunities you may wish. Without your health, your options will be limited and your outlook could be much less positive.

Having said all that, I want to encourage you not to take on too much! I know several retired leaders who took the idea of having a proactive retirement plan a little too far, and ended up getting themselves over-committed and busier than they wanted to be. So, it's about taking a thoughtful, strategic approach to post-work life, including building in plenty of time for relaxation and not saying yes to every opportunity.

As Lanse Crane, former CEO of Crane & Company, suggested in our conversations, "I am a believer that you don't always need to know what's next. Take a breath and feel settled before moving on to the next thing." Wise words, indeed.

Notes

1. As cited in Robert Kegan and Lisa Laskow Lahey, *Resistance to Change: How to Overcome It and Unlock the Potential in Yourself and Your Organization* (Harvard Business Press, Cambridge, 2009). This is a great reference on the factors that make change difficult, and how to address many of them.
2. As cited in Schumpter, J. Capitalism, Socialism and Democracy (Harper & Brothers, New York, 1942).
3. Questionnaire adapted from instrument used by Professor T.J. Jenney, Purdue University, www.tech.purdue.edu/ols/courses/ols386/crispo/changereadinesstest.doc (accessed April 19, 2017).
4. For the original research on the Big 5 personality traits, see Paul Costa and Robert McCrae, "Four Ways Five Factors Are Basic," *Personality and Individual Differences*, June 1992, 13(6), pp. 653–665.
5. As suggested by Peter Buffet, *Life Is What You Make It*, Three Rivers Press, New York, 2010.
6. G. Johns and A. Saks, *Organizational Behaviour: Understanding and Managing Life at Work*, 5th Edition. Toronto, ON: Addison Wesley Longman, 2001.
7. Adapted from scales described by Hao Zhao and Scott E. Seibert in "The Big Five Personality Dimensions and Entrepreneurial Status: A Meta-Analytic Review," *Journal of Applied Psychology*, 91(2), pp. 259–271.
8. H. Zhao and S. Seibert, "The Big 5 Personality Dimensions and Entrepreneurship: A Meta-Analytical Review," *Journal of Applied Psychology*, March 2006, 91(2), pp. 259–271.
9. For the original, groundbreaking psychology research on loss-aversion, see Daniel Kahneman and Amos Tversky, "Prospect Theory: An Analysis of Decision under Risk," *Econometrica*, March 1979, 47(2), pp. 263–291.
10. Erik Erikson, *The Life Cycle Completed*, 9th ed. (Norton, New York, 1997, p. 66).
11. D. Carmelli, A. Dame, G. Swan, and R. Rosenman, "Long-term Changes in Type A Behavior: A 27-year Follow-up of the Western Collaborative Group Study," *Journal of Behavioral Medicine*, December 1991, 14(6), pp. 593–606.
12. Erik Erikson, *The Life Cycle Completed*, 9th ed. (Norton, New York, 1997).
13. Scale adapted from Desirability of Control Scale published in Jerry Burger, *Desire for Control: Personality, Social & Clinical Perspectives*, Plenum Press, 1992.

14. M. Scheier, C. Wrosch, A. Baum, S. Cohen, L. Martire, K. Matthews, R. Schulz, & B. Zdaniuk, "The Life Engagement Test: Assessing Purpose in Life," *Journal of Behavioral Medicine*, 2006, 29(3), pp. 291–298.
15. C. Wrosch, M. Scheier, C. Carver, & R. Schulz, "The Importance of Goal Disengagement in Adaptive Self-regulation: When Giving Up is Beneficial," *Self and Identity*, 2003, 2, pp. 1–20.
16. Stephanie Brun de Pontet, *Using theories of control and self-regulation to examine the leadership transition between a parent and child in family-owned businesses*. Unpublished doctoral dissertation, Concordia University, 2008.
17. For the research background on the concept of goal reengagement, see C. Wrosch, M. Scheier, G. Miller, R. Schulz, & C. Carver, "Adaptive Self-regulation of Unattainable Goals: Goal Disengagement, Goal Re-engagement, and Subjective Well-being," *Personality and Social Psychology Bulletin*, 2003, 29, pp. 1494–1508.
18. As noted in Robert Hill, *Seven Strategies for Positive Aging*, W.W. Norton & Co., New York, 2008, p. 23.
19. Questionnaire Adapted from Goal Adjustment Capacity Scale in C. Wrosch, M. Scheier, G. Miller, R. Schulz, & C. Carver, "Adaptive self-regulation of unattainable goals: Goal disengagement, goal reengagement, and subjective well-being," *Personality and Social Psychology Bulletin*, 2003, 29, pp. 1491–1508.
20. William Bridges, *Transitions: Making Sense of Life's Changes* (Da Capo, Cambridge, 2004, p. 172).
21. A. Castonguay, C. Wrosch, and C. Sabiston, "The roles of negative affect and goal adjustment capacities in breast cancer survivors: Associations with physical activity and diurnal cortisol secretion," *Health Psychology*, 2017, 36(4), pp. 320–331.
22. Gloria Steinem, as quoted in Marc Freedman, *The Big Shift: Navigating the New Stage Beyond Midlife*, Public Affairs, New York, 2011, p. 78.

5

Is Your Family Ready for Your Transition?

As Figure 5.1 reminds us, stress or challenges in any aspect of the retiring leader's family will affect that individual's readiness for this important life transition. But it works both ways: an individual's lack of readiness for transition can contribute to stress in the family system, reducing individual-level readiness further in a cyclical way. For example, a weak marriage (family system stress) might motivate a family business CEO's spouse to discourage retirement planning, for fear that greater post-retirement focus on marriage would be stressful for both partners. The CEO may be reluctant to retire for the same reason.

In this chapter, we'll consider how the marital and broader family situation affect personal continuity, along with how good governance can smooth the path to readiness at the individual and family levels. In this context, it's important to remember how central family is to life for most of us, as a cornerstone for support and well-being. Our family members typically represent our closest personal ties and provide us a sense of connection to others and to a shared history—they provide love, purpose, and joy.

While some aspects of the traditional nuclear family have shifted over time—people marry later (if at all), have fewer children, and are increasingly part of blended families[1]—our society remains built largely around the family unit. Thus, significant life transitions such as retirement will both be affected by our family, and will have an effect on our family. This interaction may be even more pronounced in the context of a transition out of a family business, where family overlaps dramatically with that other key part of life: work.

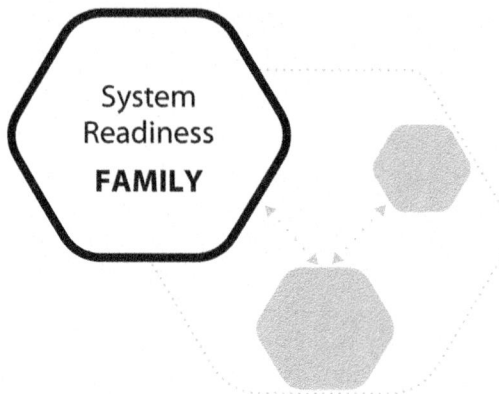

Fig. 5.1 Family readiness

Marriage/Life Partner

Your marital or life partner situation is a critical part of your plan for personal continuity. As mentioned in Chapter 4, losing your spouse can be devastating, and may be particularly hard for an individual entering a new phase of life as their business leadership career comes to a close. There is extensive research that demonstrates the positive benefits of a strong marital bond in later life. For example, research has shown that a positive marital life at age 50 was a better predictor of quality of life at age 80 than were low cholesterol levels at age 50.[2] However, even happy and healthy couples find this life-stage transition can bring unexpected challenges to their routines, their household, and their broader partnership. Let's examine factors that contribute to this.

A Common Oversight

The core family unit is built around two people who ideally share life's journey throughout adulthood. The person with whom you choose to build your life and perhaps a family will often be your closest confidant, the one who helps you talk through and navigate the big changes of life: what careers to pursue, whether to have children, where to reside, when to retire, how to spend (and save) money, and many other things. While all of these decision areas are important, those related to the work role transition is one that couples often navigate *less* in partnership than might be ideal.

While I am unaware of any research that looks at this issue directly, my own understanding and experience with client families suggests two factors likely play a role. First, retirement feels like an intensely personal change because it is related directly to your individual identity, or sense of "Who I am in the world"; second, in the context of leaving the leadership of your family's business, there are so many other stakeholders who are part of that decision that it can be easy to overlook the closest one.

In line with this, as will be discussed in greater detail in Chapter 6, many people and processes at the business need to be developed in order for a leader to successfully transition away from day-to-day management of the company. This requires work and planning on the part of the CEO and their leadership team. In addition, particularly for CEOs who have had a transformative impact on the business, there is a great deal of anxiety among employees and other key business stakeholders (banks, suppliers, customers) around how things will be different when that leader is gone. All of this is to say that the responsibilities, business issues, and stakeholders in this arena often weigh very heavily on the mind of a CEO, making it easy for them to overlook the significant change that retirement may also bring to their home life and life partner, resulting in a more difficult transition for everyone.

Potentially Conflicting Interests

In some cases, both the CEO and their spouse have formal leadership roles in the business, and there is some planning that needs to be done around both of their exits from these roles. But even setting aside the case where a spouse is also a full-time employee, there are often significant *informal* roles that the CEO's partner plays in the business and family systems. As such, some spouses may be particularly eager to leave these responsibilities behind—if they find them difficult or intrusive—and this may lead them to push their partner, the business leader, out of the leadership role more quickly or aggressively, for their own benefit.

In other situations, it's quite the opposite. I know of some families where the spouse relishes both the central decision-influencing role they carry and the ceremonial duties expected of them as part of the "first couple," and is very resistant to leaving either behind. Similarly, some CEO spouses serve as key emotional glue in multiple systems, and are valued for this role by both family and non-family leaders. In fact, the twin loss of a long-standing CEO and their partner who may also be trusted and beloved by many can exacerbate the anxiety in the system surrounding the CEO's transition out.

Now What?

In many cases, a CEO has had to invest so much time and energy in their enterprise that they may not have invested as much as they would have liked to in their marriage. Even when both partners have invested time and other resources in their relationship, there may be unspoken fears—for both of them—that they won't know what to do with one another when they suddenly have so much new "together time." If each of them has been deeply committed to efforts, work-related and otherwise, that did not involve the other very directly, they may fear they have little left in common now. Of course, this is a frequent issue not just in family business situations but in any relationship where one or both partners have immersive jobs.

Unwanted Intrusion

To carry this thinking even further, while some couples collaborate either formally or informally in the business, in other marriages each partner develops very clear and discrete spheres of influence—and any hint at overlap may not be welcome. The tongue-in-cheek expression "I married him for life, not for lunch" gets at a real fear: a partner's worry that when their spouse is no longer going into the office every day, the new retiree will upset the routines and roles their spouse or partner has developed at home or in other shared places such as a club or church.

Similar concerns I've heard expressed by partners include:

- "He is going to come home and try to be the 'boss'";
- "She is already starting to jump into my church leadership project and we don't agree on direction";
- "He is going to expect me to entertain him half the day and I have commitments and interests that still need my attention."

These are not ill-founded fears. It's true that some retired CEOs have a calendar filled with commitments that consume all the free time they thought was coming their way in retirement. But many others have spent their entire adult lives pursuing clear business goals and responding to issues and decisions brought to their attention. They have little experience identifying new, non-work projects or goals, and may really struggle to create project opportunities for themselves in outside-of-work domains. I have seen several cases of couples where the retired CEO is hoping to pursue new activities and interests with his wife, only to discover that she has plenty of activities and interests of her own that don't really involve him.

I promised my wife, 'I won't go to the grocery store with you or otherwise tell you how to be more efficient.'

PHIL CLEMENS, FORMER CEO OF CLEMENS FAMILY CORPORATION

Differences in expectations about how the couple will spend time together, engage in the community, travel, or pursue other interests can lead to real marital tension, even for otherwise very in-sync couples. Eric Allyn, co-chairman of medical equipment company Welch Allyn, for example, notes that because his wife had been in charge of the household while he was working, it took some adjustment when he was home more and able to share some of her responsibilities. Spouses really need to set aside some time, likely over a series of discussions, to level with one another about what their individual and shared vision is for their day-to-day post-retirement life. The "Talk Through Retirement with Your Partner" box on the following page provides specific tips for such a conversation (Table 5.1).

In general, a strong marriage or partnership that provides a platform for shared and individual pursuits and joys will go a long way to supporting a retiring CEO through this process. While couples can and will vary in how eager they are to spend more time together in post-work life, the key to success with this transition is *clear communication*. Take the time to think about what you want out of your partnership at this stage, and invest time in listening to your spouse to understand what their hopes are for the future as well. There is nothing to lose and everything to gain from it.

Table 5.1: Talk Through 'Retirement' with Your Partner

The main objective of a pre-retirement conversation is to get aligned on how this upcoming life phase will work for you as individuals and a couple. Approach the conversation with a spirit of partnership and mutual support, with emphasis on finding routes to shared joy. Below are more specific objectives. You are looking to build a SHARED VISION for this next phase of life.

Clarify and articulate your goals together, as related to projects, travel, service, and other significant pursuits you'd envision for this stage of life:
- What do you want to do/work on together (if anything)?
- What kind of time commitment do you expect on this?
- What other resources might this require (financial, partners, other…)?
- What role will each of you play and how will you collaborate?

Clarify and articulate your individual priorities:
- What is important to each of you in terms of projects, goals, and other issues?
- How much time will you want to spend pursuing work roles?
- How much time do you want to devote to each of your core priorities?
- What role do you want to both play in your grandchildren's lives?
- How can your spouse support you in this effort as needed?

Ensure you think about and get clear on practical matters:
- How do you understand your financial situation with end of paycheck
- What, if any, adjustments should be made to spending patterns
- How much capital do you want to set aside for philanthropy or other goals
- Talk through daily routines (sleep/wake times, shared meals, fitness activities…).

Talk through your dreams
- Where and how do you want to travel (together or individually)
- Check in on each other's 'bucket list' goals and dreams for this time…

Irv Robinson, former CEO of plastic and packaging company Robbie Fantastic Flexibles, provides a good example of how to plan ahead for the post-work phase of life with your spouse or life partner, in his quote below.

> I asked Ellen [his partner] what kind of things she wanted to be doing, how much time we would be together. It's really about envisioning the future. Just trying to learn and understand first, and then asking questions to flesh it out. Not trying to get to a conclusion or an answer, but trying to really understand where the other person is coming from in all aspects of their life, and your life with them, and not being afraid to hear the answers. Then, when you really understand where your partner is coming from you can start to conceptualize some maps - for your life, for your life together, a winning map that embraces what she wants to do, what you want to do. It's about being curious and really caring about what your partner thinks and wants.
>
> **IRV ROBINSON**, CO-FOUNDER AND FORMER CEO OF ROBBIE FANTASTIC FLEXIBLES

The "Questions to Strengthen Your Relationship" box offers queries that can help you think about how to navigate thoughtfully an impending or ongoing transition with your spouse or partner (Table 5.2).[3]

Connection with Children and Grandchildren

The nuclear family may start with a couple, but the center of gravity often shifts to children once they appear on the scene. In most cases, a retiring senior executive is not living with children at home, so the evolution in the parent–adult child relationship post-retirement is almost never as central as that described for life partners earlier in this chapter. Having said that, family members may have certain preconceived expectations about how their family may function once mom or dad is no longer as involved in day-to-day business leadership.

Let's consider some of the challenges related to the second and third generations.

>  **Table 5.2: Questions to Strengthen Your Relationship**
>
> Use the questions below to understand your partner's needs and think about practical steps each of you can take to help the other through that transition to post-work life.
>
> 1. What can I help you with right now?
> 2. How can I show you that I love you?
> 3. Is there one 'little' thing about me that you would like me to change?
> 4. Is there someplace special that you would like to go?
> 5. What is it about our life together that makes you happy?
> 6. Is there anything I can do to make you feel more loved?
> 7. What is something you'd like to do together that we have never done before?

Designated Babysitter?

I have seen multiple families where adult children with young kids of their own are hopeful that newly retired mom and dad would be able to pitch in significantly more with childcare. The motivation for this expectation may be primarily *practical*: finding a better childcare situation may free up the next generation to focus more on their career or other pursuits, while saving some money on paid help. In other cases, the objective is more *emotional*, to build strong bonds between grandparents and grandchildren. Sometimes, that latter goal is driven by the desire to give the grandchildren (third generation) the access they, the second generation, never had to their parents while growing up, due to the demands of the business. This need or hope could be present without the adult child even being aware of it, leading to intense but hard-to-explain emotions around how much time mom and dad will spend with their grandkids. Being mindful that this baggage might be present can help a family defuse the intensity of emotions here, to develop viable solutions that meet everyone's needs, with better clarity and structure regarding how much childcare the grandparents will be expected to provide.

Moreover, no matter the motivation, the idea of spending extensive time with grandchildren appeals very much to some grandparents and not so much to others. Some executives who spent years working with other adults to tackle challenging business matters absolutely relish and thrive in a child's world that is more gentle and playful and less pressure ridden; others would struggle to make that transition comfortably. This needn't be a reflection of the character or love a retired executive has for their family. Returning briefly to the notions of temperament discussed in Chapter 4, individuals come into the world with certain wiring that will make some roles more naturally comfortable than others. While it is a privilege for grandparents to really get know their grandchildren and build special bonds and memories with them, what that looks like, the time commitment that makes sense, and the flexibility that is anticipated all need to be communicated up front.

For example, Marilyn Carlson Nelson, former chair and CEO of Carlson, spoke of her and her husband's tradition of taking each grandchild on a "big trip" just for that particular child once they reached age 12. From Egypt to Madagascar and New Zealand, not only did these travels make possible remarkable grandparent–grandchild memories, but occurring as they did at a highly teachable time in the grandchildren's lives, these travels provided another way of "imprinting" family values expressed in unique settings and also helped each grandchild see themselves in the context of a larger, more complex world. This is an example of a nice, "plannable," circumscribed way to ensure quality grandparent–grandchild time.

But remember, just because a parent is leaving their day-to-day leadership of the business does not mean they are going to be entirely free of commitments. As is advocated throughout this book, we want to see transitioning leaders embrace new challenges and responsibilities (which can certainly include the care of grandchildren) that consume much of their time, thoughts, and energy. So, it's about making *mindful, intentional* choices here, as with all other elements covered in the book.

Feared Loss of Connection with Family Employees and the Business

Sometimes, the demand for shared time and attention goes the other way: that is, the retiring family member may lean on their children involved in the business to help them maintain a strong connection to both family and the business. Many retiring family business executives have had the pleasure of getting to collaborate with some or all of their children at work for years before they transition out of the leadership position—and they may miss this family and professional bond when they are no longer in daily contact at work. While there are plenty of situations where the younger generation will reach out regularly to their parent for ongoing counsel or input on key business matters post mom or dad's retirement—there are also many situations where the next generation wants to make a cleaner break, to really assert their leadership, or may be so buried in daily responsibilities that they do not think to pick up the phone much to connect with the retired parent.

This loss can feel very significant to a retiring leader, and it's important to talk through how the people involved will manage this to the mutual satisfaction of all parties. Certainly, we see many cases where the retired CEO is still connected to the business as chairman of the board or in some other formal advisory capacity. While that may keep them broadly current, that is *not* the same thing as being in the trenches every day and sitting side by side with a family member solving challenges and developing strategies. Successful businesspeople typically love the work of going into battle for market share or developing the latest innovation in their industry, and having the privilege of doing this in close collaboration with your kids can be a thrill that is hard to replicate.

But proceed carefully on this terrain. While continuing to involve the retired CEO in some strategic planning sessions or a key management decision may bring wisdom and insight from their experience, this is tricky to pull off without causing confusion around who is in charge or running the risk that a new generation of leaders will defer to their seniors rather than advance their own, potentially very valuable ideas and opinions.

This risk is even more acute in a family business setting where a family member is stepping into the shoes and shadow of a parent who may have had a transformative impact on the business, such as a charismatic founder or long-standing leader.

Because of my years and years of being the CEO, the children [who worked in the business] had an almost unhealthy reliance on me. So, my transition out was a fearful experience for my family, and I regret that.

JACK HERSCHEND, FORMER CEO OF HERSCHEND ENTERTAINMENT

It is particularly important in these transitions that the next generation feels empowered to develop their own vision and imprint on the business. Ideally, that vision is anchored in the learning and guidance from the past but independent and innovative enough to represent the direction the business needs for the future. A challenge is there may be some next-generation leaders who resist seeking their parent's good counsel on business issues for fear that it will preclude them from asserting their own direction and ideas for the enterprise.

So how do you balance these competing challenges of staying connected to the business while leaving room for others to grow into leadership roles? Here are three tips:

- *Raise greater awareness of these dynamics* to help all stakeholders appreciate the needs and concerns that may not be explicitly articulated but still play a powerful role.
- *Engage in ongoing open conversations* around what each would like to see as a balance of outreach and boundaries.
- *Develop some routines or traditions* tailored to your particular situation.

The "James and Tom Make a Plan" box illustrates these practices.

> **James and Tom Make a Plan**
>
> Early into his retirement from an industrial manufacturing business based in the US Midwest, James felt very cut off from the people with whom he had spent most of his waking hours throughout his entire adult life. He had moved his office to the family office building to minimize confusion around who was in charge, and rarely walked to the main operations building to check in or say hello. He particularly missed the daily discussions with his son Tom, the new CEO, on business issues or just the latest baseball standings.
>
> With a little urging from his wife, James spoke to his son Tom. Tom, while a very capable leader in his own right, was much less charismatic than his father. In their conversation, he shared that he had been grateful for the "clear runway" James was providing him by staying away from the office. Moreover, while Tom certainly valued his father's guidance and didn't want him to feel isolated, he was hesitant to bring him into any regular management meetings for fear this might create confusion for the team and potentially undermine his leadership, even if unintentionally.
>
> The father and son decided a good solution would be for the two of them to meet for breakfast weekly, not at work but at a restaurant in town. Beforehand, Tom would identify the topics on which he'd seek input and advice from his father; but the bulk of the time was spent catching up personally and keeping dad in the loop on the developments and people at work. The two quickly came to treasure their weekly time together, which satisfied multiple needs.

Navigating Boundaries

As the example above reminds us, the intertwining of family and business matters, along with associated relationships, is hard to disentangle. For example, while a family council—discussed below—can be a good forum for addressing family matters, it is also important to think about how these overlaps bleed into daily interactions. Similarly, a weekly parent–child breakfast to talk about business may meet the needs of both individuals around business and family connections; but it may also unintentionally distance the pair from other family members not included in the outing.

For example, in the case of James and Tom highlighted in the box, the two men are getting some quality time to connect personally that James's wife, Tom's mother, does not have with her son. She may feel motivated to encourage the extended family to have a weekly dinner, which may start to feel like a lot of family investment time to Tom, who has a young family with complicated schedules to coordinate, as well as friends with whom he wants to socialize. Like many things in life, such situations require a *trade-off*: a good solution for one need may actually create a new dilemma in the overall system. Being aware of and communicating openly about such issues is yet again the goal.

Another boundary challenge that I see become more pronounced once the senior generation has transitioned out involves keeping some family time focused *only* on family. Very often, if the retired CEO has not found an effective outlet or access to updates on the business or their former colleagues, a family dinner can rapidly devolve into "20 Questions" for the current family CEO to get their predecessor caught up on business news and issues. If everyone at the table is involved in the enterprise, this may not create any issues—but very often spouses or siblings not working in the company become frustrated by the loss of true family time.

In other cases, the successor CEO themselves may turn a family dinner into an impromptu consulting session about business matters, which may not be appreciated by others at the table, including the retired leader. Even families that have done a good job keeping family dinner focused on family for years may slip into this bad habit during this transition time if the senior generation is struggling with their need to stay in the know or the next generation uses this time to bring their parent into a business matter.

Divergent Needs for Closeness

In my experience, families that own and operate businesses together tend to be more on the "close" rather than "distant" pole when it comes to norms for family togetherness—they like being together, and make this a priority. Having said that, different family members may have varying needs on this dimension at different times, and the transition and changes that occur around the exit of one generation from leadership will thus be colored by how each individual experiences and expresses their need for closeness to family.

The psychology term sometimes used is that business-owning families tend to be more "enmeshed" (with significant ongoing contact and reliance on one another for support) rather than more "disengaged" (where family members want and have limited contact with one another).[4] While these close connections are often a source of strength, the resulting family norms can make some of the evolution of roles that accompany a leadership transition particularly challenging—especially if for some family members this change represents an opportunity to redefine boundaries to better suit their needs or preferences.

For instance, it is not unusual that a spouse who has married into this system finds the closeness or expectations for "family bonding" a bit suffocating. Thus, their hope might be that the departure of the senior generation from leadership will reduce the frequency of boundary-crossing, such as calls during dinner, unannounced visits, and the expectation that all vacations be spent with the full family. While a desire to establish some new standards on privacy and boundaries may be reasonable, seeking to alter the family interaction norms at the same time that the business leadership structure is changing may make a difficult situation even more challenging for a retiring CEO. If all the people involved can reflect on the many changes this situation is leading to for everyone else, it may lead to sufficient empathy and patience to guide an evolution that considers the needs of all.

The "Manage the Togetherness-Individuality Paradox with Care" box provides some tips for handling tensions between those who prefer ongoing closeness and those who desire more space. Since it's virtually impossible for family enterprise members to all want the same level of togetherness or intimacy, the group needs to manage the "togetherness-individuality" paradox with care, seeing it as a "both-and" rather than an "either-or." Those who prefer more personal space are often seen as not fitting in or even as trouble-makers, especially if they married into the family. Even blood relatives can diverge dramatically on this dimension, though, such as the difference between children who have moved far from the family and maintain little contact, versus those who stayed nearby and help to carry on family traditions. In many instances where togetherness needs vary, neither side shows much empathy for the other, and tensions rise. So, it's important that everyone invest time and effort into understanding others' points of view, for the collective good, including during times of transition (see Table 5.3 for suggestions on this).

Table 5.3: Manage the Togetherness-Individuality Paradox with Care

The families I've observed who do this particularly well show several common traits and behaviors:

1. *Invest in onboarding new family members:* They take care to bring in new members with a formal or informal orientation focused on what it means to join the family circle of a business family.

2. *Are comfortable with true transparency:* They demonstrate trust by sharing information about the business, along with including spouses in shared learning or philanthropy and not trying to "hide" challenging family or business issues from certain members.

3. *Appreciate other ways of 'being a family':* They recognize that how they choose to interact is not the only way for families to be, making them more open to the ideas and opinions of new family members such as in-laws.

4. *Foster acceptance:* They truly embrace a 'live and let live' mentality, even when it comes to differing needs for and interest in togetherness, such that natural, healthy divergence on this dimension is not seen as a 'problem' to be decried or fixed, but met with unconditional acceptance and positive regard.

In sum, the best way to ensure your family system is ready for your transition and can help manage it well once it's in progress, including with regard to closeness, is to *communicate* fully about expectations, hopes, and fears. As Dick DeVos, former president of direct-selling business Amway, suggests, "Transparency in the process with family is important. Families can waste a lot of time fighting shadow issues that aren't real issues—transparency will at least surface issues that are real and need to be addressed."

Good Governance Eases the Transition

In many of the examples offered so far, I've emphasized the need for greater awareness, communication, and focus on solutions that satisfy everyone's needs in the time of transition. A good governance system can be critical for promoting all of these within the family, identifying and addressing the needs of all stakeholders. More specifically, *any* family business that involves more than three shareholders should benefit from a family council, a group dedicated to managing family priorities, planning, concerns, and communication.

A family council typically involves all adult family stakeholders (whether they work in the business or not), and is the group that guides family education, retreats, policies, philanthropy, and more. Many other books provide an excellent summary of the broad role and function of a family council,[5] so here I will focus on the specific ways such a council may play a role in the planning, communicating, and supporting of the senior generation's exit from day-to-day leadership, as described in the following sections.

Promote Communication

It's critical to have a forum (such as a family council or regular family meetings) where all family stakeholders can be kept in the loop around the planning for a family leader's transition. In my experience, few things create as much angst and negative feelings as when family stakeholders find out about issues or changes in the business that are important to them from a *third party*, rather than directly from family members involved.

The discussion of a possible change in leadership is a great example of something important for family members to know about—even if they aren't shareholders or involved in the business and have no active say in the process. The last thing you want is for Suzie to hear about her brother Tim's possible replacement from a neighbor in the grocery store, or from the newspaper (I've seen this happen !). This is true even if the successor is a foregone conclusion, but it may be particularly damaging if there is a perception that there are potential family "contenders" for leadership roles in transition (e.g., maybe Suzie's feels her daughter would have been in the running "if she had ever been given half a chance to demonstrate her abilities") or if the business is seriously considering a non-family CEO for the first time.

While the choice of successor candidates is not up to the family, lack of transparency and communication on such topics leads to family members' feeling disrespected and will almost certainly erode trust. This can be toxic to the eventual successor, who will face a base of shareholders and other family members who may perceive that his or her ascension into this role was ill-conceived or inappropriate. Talk about starting off on the wrong foot!

Set Policy and Parameters

Many families work with management or the board to develop policies around opportunities for employment and advancement for family members within the enterprise. Some families reserve certain leadership roles for family members; in this case, it's important that all family members understand these rules and believe they are being applied fairly. If the broader group of family stakeholders feels significant anxiety around any proposed successor, whether it's a family member people remain unconvinced is up to the job or a proven outsider, they may put a lot of pressure on the process or resist the senior leader's exit, which will complicate a smooth transition.

Ideally, discussion about the characteristics and capabilities shareholders might expect of their business leader will be held well *before* a transition of this nature is considered—because if the process is underway, some stakeholders may feel that criteria have been developed unfairly to support or suppress specific candidate options. Similarly, if an anticipated change in leadership calls a written policy or unspoken norm into question (e.g., only family members or only males will lead), it is particularly important that family stakeholders be consulted, to promote full consideration of any trade-offs and concerns. The family council is typically the right forum for these discussions, and the right group to draft policy amendments for proposal to the board.

Guide, Education, and Preparation

The family council can also help educate family stakeholders about issues and trends in the industry that may point to the type of candidate best suited to lead the enterprise next. If ongoing family leadership of the business is a priority, the family council can, in collaboration with the business's HR group and board, ensure family members rising in the enterprise are getting the right training and experiences to groom them for future leadership roles.

Families will often invite senior executives to make a presentation on the business or industry to the family council or at a family meeting. In this context, it may be wise to begin to expose the family to prospective successors early in their career, rather than just before or after succession takes place. The more time the prospective successor has spent with the family (especially if they are a non-family executive) and the more they have demonstrated their professional capabilities through presentations and other interactions, the higher the family's confidence will be in the transition and future leader.

Facilitate Multiple Leadership Roles

Another challenge we see in family business leadership transitions is that the business leader is often also the official or de facto leader in parts of the system other than the business. They are commonly the family patriarch—that is, a leader of the family—and may even be the family council chair, another key role. Moreover, as they are often a significant shareholder in the enterprise, the retiring CEO may hold a leadership role in the ownership circle and board of directors, and might also play key roles related to family philanthropy and still other domains. While we do encourage families to find and develop different leaders for these various responsibilities, in practice there are many systems where the CEO's influence is profound throughout, given their personality, capabilities, and experience.

Thus, as the CEO moves out of business leadership, it may be a good thing (for continuity and their own well-being) that they continue to be active in other leadership roles, such as board chairman. In other cases, the business leadership transition should serve as a reminder that next-generation talent needs to be developed in all spheres, with continuity planning for leadership led by the family council and board.

Even in cases where the retiring CEO will retain other leadership roles, some planning is needed to address the transition of information flow, at the very least. The family council needs regular updates from the business leader. When the leader of both systems is the same person, that's easy enough to accomplish; but when the family chair is no longer at the helm of the business, a process for updating the family should be formalized.

Jim Ethier, former Chairman & CEO of food-processing business Bush Brothers & Company, speaks of how valuable their family senate—effectively a family council—has been in navigating challenging leadership transitions, including his own. "The Senate has been focused on education and 'keeping family at the table,'" he explains. For example, the governance group helps members of the fourth and fifth generations (including potential successors) gain family business knowledge through university-run governance and leadership programs, along with working with the family on their vision for the future, ensuring Jim didn't have to handle such large-scale tasks on his own.

Assess Your Family's Readiness and Strengthen Weak Bonds

Now that you have a better idea of the specific transition-related issues that may arise in your family system, think through your family's readiness using the informal assessment in Table 5.4. In answering, think about the concerns those around you may have, along with the intensity of their feelings. You want to evaluate how ready you think each of these stakeholders are for this

Table 5.4: Assessing Family Stakeholder Readiness

Please use the below to assess the extent to which you believe various stakeholders feel 'ready' for your eventual transition out of the leadership role.

STAKEHOLDER GROUPS	GENERAL LEVEL of 'READINESS' or COMFORT with TRANSITION	VIEW OF BUSINESS GOING FORWARD...	IMPACT of TRANSITION on PERSONAL RELATIONSHIP	IDEAS ON ADDRESSING CONCERNS
CURRENT GENERATION				
Your spouse	High (calm) Uncertain Low (worried)	Good Unsure Worried	Will improve Unsure Will strain	
Sibling Shareholders (if any)	High (calm) Uncertain Low (worried)	Good Unsure Worried	Will improve Unsure Will strain	
Other (fill in)	High (calm) Uncertain Low (worried)	Good Unsure Worried	Will improve Unsure Will strain	
NEXT GENERATION				
Your children working in business (if any)	High (calm) Uncertain Low (worried)	Good Unsure Worried	Will improve Unsure Will strain	
Your children not working in business (if any)	High (calm) Uncertain Low (worried)	Good Unsure Worried	Will improve Unsure Will strain	
Other family working in business (if any)	High (calm) Uncertain Low (worried)	Good Unsure Worried	Will improve Unsure Will strain	
Other family shareholders	High (calm) Uncertain Low (worried)	Good Unsure Worried	Will improve Unsure Will strain	
Other (fill in)	High (calm) Uncertain Low (worried)	Good Unsure Worried	Will improve Unsure Will strain	

Table 5.5: Tips on a 'Reset' to Strengthen Family Bonds

1. Acknowledge the history
   - Acknowledge your time imbalance of the past
   - Ask to hear how this impacted family members—what they missed or were frustrated by
   - Share what you feel you missed

2. *Share your goals to connect differently*
   - Share your hopes for a stronger bond and ask how that will be received
   - Explain that you hope to 'show up differently' and that can take some getting used to for everyone...
   - Set realistic expectations as to what that change could look like and time needed for evolution – ask for help and support through this effort
   - Get aligned on boundaries and preferred communication (email, phone, text)

3. *Seek and nurture common interests*
   - Be curious about what is important in the life of each family member
     - Express interest in their priorities
     - Seek ways to support these as appropriate, or of shared interest
   - Seek common interests and share experiences around these, such as:
     - Time at a ball game with grandchildren
     - Great dining
     - Tennis/golf/other sport
     - Volunteering on a community project together
     - Trips to go skiing/boating/other activity
   - Suggest family holidays and trips (let others take the lead on where and what)

4. *Reach out in a committed, consistent way*
   - Remember your adult children's lives are very busy – don't let that derail you
   - Establish routines or traditions that fit for all (weekly call, meal, annual trip)
   - Do things that they need and value
   - Find ways to connect one-on-one as well as with individual family units or full family gatherings

5. *Leverage family gatherings appropriately*
   - Ensure you don't spend all your time focused on business updates at retreats
   - Make sure there is enough open time at family meetings for just hanging out
   - Advocate for fun activities that engage the whole family and create great memories

transition, that is, how comfortable are they with you stepping out of leadership and the next generation taking over. You want to further think about their confidence in the future of the business—are they generally positive about where things are going, unsure, or very worried. Finally, consider how this transition, combined with their sense of readiness or not, will impact your personal bond with them. In other words, will this process add to stress between you, or is this an opportunity to strengthen your bonds with this person? Finally, the last column is critical, as it's a place to note ideas for how to address the issues indicated here, including using the ideas in this book.

The assessment above and other indicators may point to strains within the family due to your current or past leadership role. After all, it's not uncommon that a business leader has had to sacrifice a lot of time with family to achieve the success they have in business. Sometimes this will lead to more impoverished relationships with adult children than is ideal. In Table 5.5, as a final tool for this chapter, are tips for how to address this challenge.

Notes

1. See, for example, Jens Manuel Krogstad, "5 Facts About the Modern American Family," *Pew Research Center Fact Tank*, April 30, 2014, http://www.pewresearch.org/fact-tank/2014/04/30/5-facts-about-the-modern-american-family/ (accessed January 31, 2017).
2. As cited in George Vaillant, *Aging Well*, Little, Brown and Co., Boston, 2002, p. 13.
3. Questions from Barton Goldsmith, "7 Questions That Can Strengthen Your Relationship," *Psychology Today*, August 6, 2014, https://www.psychologytoday.com/blog/emotional-fitness/201408/7-questions-can-strengthen-your-relationship (accessed April 25, 2017).
4. "Enmeshment" has often been used to describe family systems marked by excessively close relationships and dependence among members, reflecting a sort of systemic pathology. Here, I'm using the term more generally to denote families that prioritize togetherness, sometimes at the expense of other important individual or collective pursuits.
5. See, for example, the very useful book by Chris Eckrich and Steve McClure, *The Family Council Handbook*, Palgrave Macmillan, New York, 2012.

6

Is Your Business Ready for Your Transition?

When Dave Juday was named CEO of Ideal Industries, a test and measurement equipment company, at age 39, he sat down at the desk that had been his father's, ceremoniously threw out all his dad's pencils, and replaced them with his own. Then he leaned back in his chair and said to himself, "What do I do now?" Years later, as he started to work on his own transition planning, he knew he didn't want his successor to have that same experience.

What Juday and other incoming leaders quickly recognize is that the health and stability of their family firm at the point they become responsible for it influences their transition into the role. Likewise, the current state of the business also enables the outgoing leader to depart with less (or more) anxiety about what will happen to the company in their absence. That is, having a stable business typically helps the leader let go of their (often longtime) role and move on to other pursuits, while enabling successors to start strong. As Fig. 6.1 suggests, your internal readiness to make the transition is not independent of the state of the business at the time of your planned departure—recall from Chapter 5 that this was the case for the family system as well.

In other words, any significant stress in, or on the business, will affect the individual's readiness, and vice versa. There are many ways in which this can happen. For example, lack of financial stability within the business would naturally increase stress for the outgoing CEO—with regard to both their own financial security and their concerns for the longevity of the company. Further, a struggling business provides the perfect "excuse" for a leader already ambivalent about their departure to slow down the transition process or boomerang back into key decisions because they perceive—whether accurately or not—that the business needs rescuing. Similarly, lack of alignment around

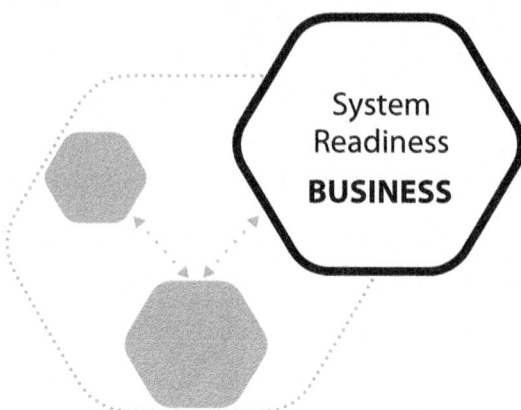

Fig. 6.1 Business readiness

the future of the enterprise from next-generation owners can create a vacuum of ideas and direction that may motivate people to draw back in a leader who is on the verge of exit or who has already departed the enterprise.

In short, those without sufficient personal readiness are more likely to get overly involved in the details of the business, even if they are near the end of their tenure. On the other hand, even leaders who are truly ready to depart their role and have planned well ahead to prepare the business for their exit may face challenges to leaving because economic (such as competition or loss of revenues) or talent-related (such as lower-performing potential successors or leadership teams) issues "pull" for them to remain at the enterprise to help weather the storm.

This chapter will discuss "business readiness" in detail at the *enterprise* and *individual* (i.e., successor) levels. Note that because much has been written about some of the family business topics here—including succession and governance—I will stick to covering the ground most relevant to issues of personal readiness and transition, and refer you to helpful resources for a more general treatment of other ideas and practices, where relevant.

Enterprise Readiness

It's easy to focus on readiness at the individual level—for both the departing and incoming leaders. But, in reality we need to think much more broadly, as the entire *enterprise* goes through a transition when the top leader departs. What kind of ownership group, management bench, governance system, and other organization-level structures and processes will best support the successor and other stakeholders including owners? This section examines each element of that question in detail.

Aligned and Committed Ownership: With a Vision for the Future

Especially in the context of a transition, owners have to be clear on the *job of the owner*. Do they understand the responsibility of ownership and do they have the knowledge needed to do this job well? If not, they will need to go through education to better learn the role.

A major responsibility of ownership is setting the vision for the ownership group and enterprise. Too often, this responsibility is overlooked, for two reasons:

- *Mistaking past for future*: People assume the vision of the past will be the vision for the future, which may or may not make sense depending on the needs, goals, and priorities of next-generation owners, along with marketplace realities related to demand, competition, supply chain, and other factors;
- *Apathy*: Even a well-intentioned group of owners can become apathetic or indifferent to development of a collective vision, due to distance from the enterprise and one another—as is often the case in later generations, when members tend to be dispersed across different geographies, cultures, and mindsets. More on this follows soon.

In this context, each generation of owners has to answer one critical question: why? Why do they want to be partners with one another, and what is their shared vision for the enterprise? Answering that requires owners to understand and be able to articulate their ownership goals, with genuine alignment around these. The "Owners Must Grapple with GRPL" box provides more detail on the specific goals owners have to consider.

> **Owners Must Grapple with GRPL**
>
> Family business owners need to think about their collective goals in four key areas of the enterprise, to help inform management decisions and ensure the board is keeping shareholder interests in mind. The four areas represent the acronym "GRPL," as described below:
>
> *Growth*: Where, how, and at what pace do we want to grow—geographically, product line, horizontal or vertical integration—and what information can we provide, mostly through the board, to help management align strategy with our growth goals?
>
> *Risk*: What kind of financial and other risk are we willing to take, and what are the boundaries of our comfort zone on these?
>
> *Profits*: What kind of return do we realistically expect from the business?
>
> *Liquidity*: What are our expectations for dividends and liquidity events, including to address the needs of those who wish to depart ownership (redemption of shares)?

Once owners articulate a clear view of their goals and the vision these feed into, they can answer another key question: Does their vision for the future make them buyers or sellers? That gets at their level of commitment—or lack thereof. Next-generation owners who are eager to steward the legacy built by prior generations—what we could consider "buyers" here, or committed owners—have a strong sense of psychological ownership and, typically, good clarity on what their legacy will be. This provides a strong "scaffolding" for a leadership transition, such that the outgoing leader feels comfortable about the business's longevity and the incoming one has clear direction from the owners.

But that doesn't mean it will be an easy transition in every case. For example, the ownership group may have a clear, collective vision for the future but be only comfortable with the *outgoing* leader at the helm. Thus, a level of comfort and confidence in the incoming leader on the part of the ownership group will also smooth the transition, as discussed later in this chapter.

Note also that the rise of next-generation leaders often accompanies an expansion in the ownership group in terms of sheer numbers, as the enterprise moves from founders to siblings to generations of cousins. As suggested above, a dispersed ownership group can be difficult to keep engaged and emotionally invested as *stakeholders* on multiple dimensions, rather than just financially invested as stockholders. In this case, ensuring that processes are well developed (such as through visioning exercises led by family leaders and outside advisors) to get owners on the same page regarding their vision for the enterprise and to communicate that vision to the board, and thus to company leadership, is critical to support a near-term or future transition. (For more information on the role of owners in a family business, please refer to *Family Business Ownership*, by Aronoff and Ward.)

Stable Position in Market

A second business-system factor that will affect any leadership transition has to do with *stability*. That includes the ability to answer questions like these positively, with confidence:

- Is the company poised for profitable growth in a fast-evolving marketplace?
- Has the business kept pace with competitors on the dimensions of products, services, and talent to meet ongoing market demands?
- Have key relationships with vendors, banks and creditors, investors, and customers remained relevant, with management of these by leaders other than the retiring CEO alone?

At any time, but especially in the face of a transition, it's critical for leaders to understand the health of the business on a set of key metrics. The exact set may vary from company to company but will generally include dimensions pointed to by the questions above. I've found Michael Porter's well-known "5 Forces Model" to be helpful in thinking about where the business stands. His model includes these dimensions:[1]

- *Supplier Power*: How dependent are you on suppliers for key inputs? How many suppliers provide the inputs you need (the more, the better)? Would it be easy for suppliers to demand higher prices or other terms that are not in your favor?
- *Buyer Power*: How large and diverse is your customer pool (the larger and more diverse, the better)? How easy is it for them to switch to your rivals (the harder, the better)?
- *Competition*: What is the number, capability, and quality of your competitors? How actively are rivals going after your customers and market share? What are opportunities to partner with competitors, if any?
- *Threat of Substitution*: What options do customers have to avoid buying the products and services you offer altogether, such as creating their own in-house or through outsourcing?
- *Barriers to Entry*: How easy is it for new competitors to enter your market space? What costs and other barriers—such as those related to technology, talent, or regulations—might keep new rivals out, making it easier for you to maintain a favorable market position?

Financial Strength

Financial stability is of course critical for any business. Questions related to growth and profitability, cash reserves, creditworthiness, free cash flow, and many other financial dimensions must be answered positively to promote confidence in an imminent leadership transition. Executive leadership will guide financial strategy and initiatives, and "best practices" exist for any financial tactic, but as with anything, real-world considerations must help shape financial approaches. For example, as discussed earlier, owners need to provide clear inputs on their expectations for liquidity in the form of dividends.

Similarly, the outgoing CEO and their successor (if also a family member) may likely be significant shareholders with high personal stakes in the business's financial health. Thus, they will be very focused on financial strength, as it relates directly to their future, whether near term (for the outgoing leader) or most distantly (for the successor). "The Power of One More Zero" box provides a key insight on how some people think about their personal finances, which can affect the timing and smoothness of transition.

> **The Power of One More Zero**
>
> What does it take for people to feel financially comfortable, both in terms of their present and future? The reality is that the majority of households in the USA *don't* feel financially secure—and most couldn't even come up with an extra $400 easily for an emergency.[2] But even much better-off households, including those occupied by family business members or leaders, tend to believe that they need significantly larger assets to feel secure about their financial future.
>
> While different people will answer "How much money do you need to feel secure?" very differently, I've found that many of those in family business need effectively "another zero" in their net worth (10 times its current value) to feel comfortable with the future. That's true across the scale: if they are currently worth $3 million, they'd like to be worth closer to $30 million; if they're worth $20 million, they'd be comfortable closer to 10 times that amount, or $200 million! Of course, we can debate how much money people *really* need to feel secure—most over- or underestimate—but the key point here is that it takes a *lot* of assets for most of us to feel comfortable retiring, and that can influence a family business leadership transition, especially if the financial health of the business is in question.

More practically, keep in mind that the departing leader will often maintain some level of ownership after they retire, so they are tethered in a very material way to the business's performance. In some cases, the income stream from this investment may represent a significant portion (or all) of their retirement income. In other cases, transitioning CEOs expect to earn a "pension," "consulting fee," or get "bought out" from proceeds of the business over time in their retirement. As a result of this financial interconnection, if the economic stability of the business makes these planned-for income streams unrealistic, many leaders will delay their exit. Alternatively, if a leader has exited but then finds weaker performance of the business puts much of their planned income at risk, they could feel a lot of personal pressure to jump back in to try to right the ship. It's paramount to understand the expectations of the leader and broader shareholder group as related to these issues.

Having an enterprise that is financially stable and sustainable not only reassures the leader that they can let go ("My baby is in good shape"), but it may also enable greater financial returns and opportunities for that leader ("I can do more things that require money"), whether related to philanthropy, a new venture, or some other major undertaking they want to pursue post business leadership. Ideally, the business would have sufficient access to liquidity to buy out the interest of the departing leader over time, to reduce their personal exposure to the enterprise's financial ups and downs.

Financial security can also provide a leader with the means to pursue some of those other meaningful goals we have been advocating throughout this book.

> There is nothing that is more rewarding than having had the privilege of helping my dad come to end of his life gracefully and achieve some of the things he wanted to do. He wanted to make a contribution in education but didn't have the background or horsepower in later life - so he and I worked together on some amazing projects. The last thing we did was to create an entrepreneurship class. The idea was that anybody who wanted to start a company would take this 12-week class and would get the background and knowledge – and it turned out to be a wildly successful program.
>
> Then, a lot of the people coming out of the class would have no place to start their business. I got very close to the school in Northern Wisconsin – so, I bought a factory building and called it a manufacturing incubator. It is a public private partnership - 1 am the private, I own the building & eat all the losses. The local economic development corp. is the public in this really depressed area. I am up there about half the time and it is just wonderful fun to make all new kinds of friends and operate and schmooze with people like the economic development corp. players. For me, I wouldn't have had this opportunity if I hadn't had the opportunity to work with my dad in his waning years - because I was helping dad put his money into the community. He and I worked together on these things - so I knew what he wanted. It was based on that experience and the work I did with economic development in Illinois & the thing that was playing to my strength: background in manufacturing.
>
> **DAVID JUDAY,** FORMER CEO OF IDEAL INDUSTRIES

Sustainable Structures and Processes

The "readiness" of the business can be meaningfully improved by the presence of a number of business and oversight structures. Let's consider three central structures and processes that promote smoother transition: governance, leadership team, and strategic planning.

Governance and Oversight

If there's no corporate board in place, an imminent leadership transition can make the need to develop one particularly urgent. This is in part because a board can play a critical role in supporting the transition process for the departing leader, providing a strong source of accountability and empathy during this important and often challenging process. (For a more comprehensive treatment on the benefits and processes to put a board in place, please refer to our book *Building a Successful Family Business Board* by Pendergast, Ward, and Brun de Pontet).

Moreover, because the board protects the interests of *all* shareholders—even if a departing leader may have not wanted or needed a board—stakeholders may be far more comfortable with transition if there is a strong board in place for oversight and continuity. If the incoming leader is the first non-family leader, shareholders may feel especially reassured by the presence of a board that will hold management accountable and ensure the voice, values, and culture of the family remain considered at the highest levels. On a more practical note, the discipline needed to prepare for board meetings will strengthen the reporting and communication channels for stakeholders, ensuring greater distribution of more comprehensive information about business performance and leadership decisions.

Even when a board is present, it can very much be the *outgoing* leader's board. Thus, it's wise to consider a younger board that can support and evolve with the new leader. "Does the profile of the board continue to fit the needs of the business?" is the critical question to ask, as related to how well the board's structure and the directors' profiles fit the business's purpose and mission, the needs of rising-generation shareholders, and the new leadership team. Examine the board carefully in this context, and be willing to make necessary changes. That being said, it's important not to try to change *everything* at once: If the board in place is working well, that body can help the outgoing senior leader make the often-difficult transition by providing empathy and feedback, as mentioned earlier. The next generation of leaders, in turn, will benefit from a board representing a greater mix of generations and viewpoints. Think of it as aiming for enough of an old guard to support the outgoing leader's departure, along with an emphasis on recruiting new blood to support and add value to new leaders' plans and perspective. Thus, an effective, diverse board acts as both a strong support for the transition and a stable bridge to new leadership.

> My board pushed me to leave 'all the way' - to not serve on the board at all. I didn't appreciate that at the time, but it helped with a healthy separation for me and for the business.
>
> **LANSE CRANE,** FORMER CEO, CRANE & COMPANY

Finally, clear policies around board term limits can help the enterprise and outgoing/incoming leaders alike plan for transitions, as Phil Clemens, former CEO of the Clemens Family Corporation, suggests:

We have age limits. As of age 62 you can stay on the board but the board has to approve it and 65 is our mandatory retirement age. In my late 50s the board said they wanted me to stay on until I was 65, and we began to plan for my succession in earnest. We had decided my successor several years in advance, and that allowed us to communicate with stakeholders and actively start to transition the roles and responsibilities.

PHIL CLEMENS, FORMER CEO OF CLEMENS FAMILY CORPORATION

Likewise, as Marilyn Carlson Nelson, former chair and CEO of Carlson, stated, "It's hard to stay on the board past being the chair or CEO. It's hard when you feel strongly about things but times change. Sometimes our stories [as outgoing leaders] are less valuable than we think."

Strong Leadership Team with Proven Members

Leadership continuity should be planned proactively throughout the enterprise, with a clear sense of the roles needed to drive the business forward and maintenance of a team of capable and trusted leaders who can execute well, along with an established process to recruit to fill gaps as needed. Despite what may seem like best efforts, the risk remains that when a senior leader retires, he is surrounded by a similar-aged group also approaching retirement. If there hasn't been much planning over the past five to ten years, there can be excessive turnover among leadership, leading to a damaging cumulative loss of institutional knowledge, key relationships, coaches and mentors, and the like. Planning the broader leadership transition carefully, then, is paramount.

How can you do this well? Largely by asking questions including about how long the current CEO wishes to work. But it's not just about the CEO: As any senior leader transitions, they leave their position open, requiring sequential filling of roles with well-qualified people. For example, the current CEO may be replaced by the CFO, leaving that CFO position vacant;

then, if the comptroller or some other financial manager moves into the CFO position, their previous position will have to be filled, and so on. Do a deep dive on such planning by collecting opinions and real estimates on tenure, then develop a calendar of transition points based on the information gathered.

As you embark on any such effort, remember that people don't always want to think about retirement; it can be uncertain and scary for anyone. That means it may be easier for leaders to address end-of-tenure questions as part of a company-wide initiative as suggested above, rather than making individual leaders feel singled out for the information. Statements such as "We're asking everyone 50 and older about their retirement goals" can help people feel comfortable with the effort.

In addition to understanding and planning for people's timetables, ask key questions of all relevant stakeholders (management, owners, directors, etc.) about how they feel with regard to the leadership transition, as follows.

- Does next-generation leadership have sufficient respect for the wisdom of elders (outgoing and ongoing leaders) *and* the ability to forge their own vision?
- Is everyone aligned on the leadership role of the retiring leader? For example, will he or she serve on the board as chair?
- How will the exiting leader's wisdom/experience be tapped without overshadowing or undermining new lines of reporting?

Depending on what you learn or observe, take steps to ensure a strong bridge between old and new leaders and teams. This might mean anchoring new leadership ideas and goals in established long-standing values, for example, or helping senior-generation leaders understand the value of new ideas. Support the incoming leader as needed but without coddling them or letting them get away with entitled behavior—that will lead to the loss of capable leaders and erosion of enterprise culture and performance. (For more ideas on leadership development and other human resources in family businesses broadly, please also reference *Human Resources in the Family Business* by Ransberg, Sage-Howard, and Schuman). It can also be of value to have informal or semi-formal ceremonies to pass the torch to incoming leaders, as implied by the story from Jim Ethier below.

> When I officially handed the role to Drew (next-generation family member and new board chair) I made a speech focused on the 'challenge to the next generation' and joked that all that mattered was that my assistant was there to manage the process. While it was an important moment to underscore this transition – I wanted to keep it light, to celebrate the success of this moment. To that end, I stopped at Burger King on my way to the event and got a crown to place on Drew's head as a surprise, and gave him an engraved gavel. We hit all the high notes. In fact, it was during my comments while putting the crown on cousin Drew's head that a senior member of our third generation said loudly enough to be heard by all that: "what? Succession without acrimony!
>
> **JIM ETHIER,** FORMER CHAIRMAN & CEO, BUSH BROTHERS & COMPANY

Strategic Planning Processes

Effective transition relies not just on people, but *process*. According to family business expert John L. Ward, three things are needed for successful transition:

- A board with independent directors (discussed earlier)
- A competent successor (discussed later)
- A clear strategic planning process.

This section discusses the last element in this list: strategic planning. While an outgoing founding or long-standing family business CEO may have had the flexibility to lead the business through trust, gut instinct, and less formality, the incoming leadership group will likely be heading a larger enterprise and thus require greater discipline and process around planning. A clearer, more professionalized strategic planning process helps owners and others in the enterprise feel more comfortable with broad direction and decision-making, along with more specific changes driven by new leaders. And the less central the outgoing leader is to the planning, the better for the system.

> During our last strategic planning session, I went to Key West, drank Rum and read books - it was purposeful. If I were in the room, they would all be looking at my face to see how I am reacting.
>
> JIM ETHIER, FORMER CHAIRMAN & CEO, BUSH BROTHERS & COMPANY

It can be a challenge to know where to start with planning. A critical guiding factor here is *voice*: where is the input of owners in the strategic plan, and does the board have the ability and opportunity to question the plan, rather than just rubber-stamping it?

As you can imagine, relating the owners' collective vision to the broader strategic vision for the enterprise doesn't "just happen." A robust planning process ensures effective communication, sharing of priorities/concerns/opportunities, allocation of resources, and other important activities. The owners' vision needs to be related to the business's opportunities and strategy, and the board needs to be leveraged to review, question, and refine the strategy. The board then will hold management accountable for executing on the strategy and providing updates to shareholders so they are kept in the loop—all of this takes planning. (For more details on this parallel planning process, please consult *When Family Businesses are Best* by Carlock and Ward)

Capable and Trusted Successor

Now that we've covered enterprise-level issues related to business-system readiness, let's turn to *individual* issues—namely, the presence of a trusted, capable successor, as part of an effective leadership transition. The ideal successor will have a combination of objectively proven abilities, established trust from stakeholders, and a demonstrated commitment to the family and business, as described in the sections below.

Objectively Proven Abilities

An incoming leader should be well into a credible professional development path that has helped them gain key business and leadership skills across multiple areas of real responsibility. If the next-generation successor is a family member, they will preferably have worked *outside* the business for some meaningful period of time. Working in an organization where their last name doesn't matter allows a potential successor to prove themselves in a more objective setting. This has several benefits. Success outside the family business builds the skills of the rising leader, along with their credibility in the eyes of family business owners and other constituents. Critically, it also nurtures their own confidence in their ability to lead, or self-belief. So many fledgling and established leaders—from politicians to CEOs to artists—have imposter syndrome, or the belief that they're not truly qualified for their roles and will be ultimately exposed as frauds.[3] Success outside the business can offset this all-too-common problem.

As importantly, a rising family leader has to have taken on high-stakes assignments in the business with a real possibility of *failure*, to prove their ability to navigate executive-level challenges.[4] Family firms often have a "can't fail" mentality, such that rising leaders are protected from potential failures; ironically, that results in failure to prove themselves adequately. Ideally, the prospective successor will have had a range of experiences and supervisors in work roles where their performance was easy to evaluate objectively (they had budgetary responsibility, they were accountable for winning a major account, they were responsible for profit and loss of a business unit or line, and so on).

Family business consultant Ivan Lansberg characterizes the credibility assessments a rising leader in their domain faces as the "Tests of a Prince," as described in the next box.

> **The Tests of a Prince**
>
> Lansberg identifies four different types of "tests" new family enterprise leaders must face:[5]
>
> *Qualifying tests*: These are the more "formal" criteria by which leadership capability might be judged, such as educational level and institutions, work experience, community or military service, awards and recognition won. Specific work achievements in the family firm or elsewhere also fall into this category.
>
> *Self-imposed tests*: The expectations that leaders set for themselves, and the criteria by which they expect other stakeholders to judge them. This might include items thought of as qualifying tests (above), but also how well the new leader's ideas or perspectives are received with regard to vision, strategy, and business initiatives.
>
> *Circumstantial tests*: These are the unexpected challenges that emerge for rising leaders, such as filling the shoes of a senior leader due to a health crisis, dealing with a major business disruption like the recall of a high-revenue product, or handling an unforeseen harsh regulatory measure.
>
> *Political tests*: This often takes the form of challenges from internal rivals, whether family or non-family managers. As such players maneuver for political clout, they might undermine the anointed success in various ways, such as impeding the focal leader's ideas or recruiting opposition from multiple areas. How the leader handles such political pressure will affect their credibility.

Trusted by Key Stakeholders

As the previous section suggests, a leadership transition will be smoothest when the successor has the trust of stakeholders including owners and the leadership team in place. Qualifications earned within or outside the family business help earn others' trust, as just discussed.

Yet, so do "softer" skills, especially those that fall under the umbrella of "emotional intelligence." Emotional intelligence is viewed broadly as the ability to reason about emotions and emotional information, such as:[6]

- Capacity to solve emotion-related problems effectively;
- Ability to perceive emotional facial expressions accurately;
- Understanding of one's own emotions and how these affect one's actions (sadness makes you withdraw or act irritably toward others, for example);
- Ability to manage one's own emotions well (such as not lashing out at others when frustrated about something unrelated) and respond to emotion in others helpfully (such as giving someone who appears sad more space).

Emotional intelligence, along with related traits such as humility, enables an incoming leader to develop warm, trusting, collaborative relationships with other stakeholders, including the outgoing leader, other owners, the leadership team and other employees, customers, suppliers, and many other groups. Not surprisingly, those relationships can promote better performance at the individual, team, and enterprise levels, assuming the successor has some baseline level of business skill.

In contrast, a leader who is strong on business qualifications and capabilities but *lacks* emotional intelligence, who goes about burning bridges, stepping on toes, making unilateral decisions, and generally behaving in ways that erode the trust of the family and other leaders, will generally not enjoy long-term success. Those of us who work closely with family firms have seen countless such examples, especially when the new leader in question is a family member who was handed the position rather than truly earning it.

In short, a new leader who has gained the trust of stakeholders—family, management, board, employees, community—by investing genuinely in relationships with them will make for a much more effective, healthy leadership transition.

Commitment to Family and Business

We can think of commitment to the business and family as a foundational quality of an effective incoming leader. My own doctoral research looked at this issue directly: I found that junior (future) leaders who were *intrinsically* motivated to work in the business—they were doing it because it mattered to them, not primarily for financial compensation or out of obligation to the family (both external motivators)—had retiring parent CEOs who were more confident in the rising leaders' abilities and impact.[7] In short, demonstrated commitment bred trust among important constituents.

Commitment should be evident on two important, related dimensions:

- *Family*: Commitment to the family means a dedication to helping owners develop and bring to life a clear, meaningful vision that's truly collective. It entails respecting responsibilities to the family, such as sharing updates on the business with the broad ownership group; appreciating the importance of funding the family council; and commitment to keeping the business in the family, rather than focusing on selling or going public.
- *Business*: Commitment here is about a genuine passion for the business mission and objectives but also an ability to have fun with the job, whether crafting new strategies and tactics or thinking about how best to motivate employees.

New leaders who embrace a "servant leadership" mentality are particularly likely to embody this two-pronged commitment. Servant leadership, briefly, is a focus on bringing out the best in others through active support, whether in the form of creating a trust-based culture, soliciting opinions from all quarters, providing encouragement and coaching, or acting with humility and empathy.[8] Such behavior, not surprisingly, fosters trust in others and makes them feel heard, promoting a more generally collaborative, high-energy environment important for a leadership transition.

Commitment to the family and business among successors or potential ones can also be fostered in part through mentorship by the outgoing leader. Frank Schurz, former CEO of Schurz Communication, for example, mentors his four nephews who work in the business. "I'm mentoring them more around family needs, civic engagement, things of that nature," he explains, highlighting the importance of continuity in values and culture among leaders.

Assess Your Business's and Successor's Readiness

Now that you're familiar with the facets of business system and successor readiness in regard to your transition, there follow some tools to help you evaluate each.

Your Business's Readiness

Use the scale in Table 6.1 to evaluate the "transition-readiness" and general strength of specific dimensions of your business. For this assessment and the one that follows, consult Appendix 3 for the scoring guide. As stated previously, these assessment tools are not meant to be seen as 'scientific instruments' but more as conversation starters for your planning efforts.

Pay special attention to areas you rated as being less ready, and think about how to strengthen those sooner rather than later, including by using the ideas in this chapter and elsewhere in this book.

Table 6.1: How Ready is Your Business for Transition?

Please assess your business' level of 'readiness' on the seven dimensions below.

Evaluate your business along each of these dimensions:	Score to attribute for each answer below:				
	5	4	3	2	1
Ownership Group Alignment	Very Ready	Mostly Ready	Marginally Ready	Some Steps Taken	No Progress
Company's Position in Industry	Dominant	Strong	Good	Marginal	Weak
Financial Condition of Business	Very Strong	Strong	Modest	Marginal	Weak
Successor Capability	Excellent	Very Strong	Good	Marginal	Weak
Next Generation Management Team	Excellent	Very Strong	Good	Marginal	Weak
Professional Board of Directors	Excellent & longstanding	Very good	Getting established	Informal	Weak
Written Strategic Plan	Strong & widely supported	Solid	Being developed	Rough ideas	We don't plan
SUM of POINTS: _____					

Your Successor's Readiness

Use the scale in Table 6.2 to evaluate your successor's readiness on multiple dimensions, and as above, address lower-rated areas using the ideas in this book and those from other sources.

Table 6.2: Confidence in Prospective Successor

Please review the statements below, and indicate to what degree you believe they are strengths of the prospective successor for leadership in your business:

Not at all	A little	Somewhat	A great deal	A lot
1	2	3	4	5

Making good business decisions	1 ☐	2 ☐	3 ☐	4 ☐	5 ☐
Developing a strong and empowered senior leadership team	1 ☐	2 ☐	3 ☐	4 ☐	5 ☐
Having the right experience and judgment to bring to challenging situations	1 ☐	2 ☐	3 ☐	4 ☐	5 ☐
Nurturing the culture and reputation of the business	1 ☐	2 ☐	3 ☐	4 ☐	5 ☐
Managing the company's financial health in line with strategic goals	1 ☐	2 ☐	3 ☐	4 ☐	5 ☐
Developing strong & trusting bonds with other owners	1 ☐	2 ☐	3 ☐	4 ☐	5 ☐
Effectively using the board and other key advisors	1 ☐	2 ☐	3 ☐	4 ☐	5 ☐
Growing the company					
SUM of POINTS: _____					

Notes

1. For more on Porter's 5 Forces Model see Michael Porter, *Competitive Strategy: Techniques for Analyzing Industries and Competitors*, Free Press, New York, 1998.
2. For more on the growing sense of financial insecurity in the USA (including the article author's very personal take on the situation), see Neal Gabler, "The Secret Shame of Middle Class Americans," *The Atlantic*, May 2016, http://www.theatlantic.com/magazine/archive/2016/05/my-secret-shame/476415/ (accessed February 7, 2017).
3. For more on imposter syndrome see Carl Richards, "Learning to Deal with the Imposter Syndrome," *New York Times*, October 26, 2015, https://www.nytimes.com/2015/10/26/your-money/learning-to-deal-with-the-impostor-syndrome.html (accessed February 8, 2017).
4. Developing Next Generation Leaders in a Family Business by Stephen Miller, article published by the Family Business Consulting Group. http://www.thefbcg.com/assets/1/22/FBA_Developing_Next_Generation_Leaders_SPM.pdf
5. Ivan Lansberg, "The Tests of a Prince," *Harvard Business Review*, September 2007, https://hbr.org/2007/09/the-tests-of-a-prince (accessed February 8, 2017).
6. For an overview and academic references related to emotional intelligence, see John D. Mayer, "What Emotional Intelligence Is and Is Not," *Psychology Today*, September 21, 2009, https://www.psychologytoday.com/blog/the-personality-analyst/200909/what-emotional-intelligence-is-and-is-not (accessed February 8, 2017).
7. Stephanie Brun de Pontet. *Using theories of control and self-regulation to examine the leadership transition between a parent and child in family-owned businesses.* Unpublished doctoral dissertation, Concordia University, 2008.
8. For a story-based approach to the concept of servant leadership, see James Hunter, *The Servant*, Crown Business, New York, 2008.

7

Where Are You From and Why Does That Matter?

Now that we've covered the three core parts of the model—personal readiness, family readiness, and business readiness—we turn to the broader context, as this will also play a significant role in the nature of your personal continuity and post-work life. In short, several key features of your social and physical environment will influence your experience, whether explicitly or in subtler ways. Figure 7.1 illustrates how the processes we have described to date occur within a context (geographic, cultural, etc.) that influences each part of the model.

This idea relates to the broader theme we've discussed throughout this book: life and change don't happen in a vacuum. That includes your transition from day-to-day leadership. So, in this chapter, we'll look beyond the systems and individuals directly impacted by this transition to the broader context, including the social/cultural norms that predominate where you're from (locally and nationally), along with your existing experience base and the people and physical space that surround you.

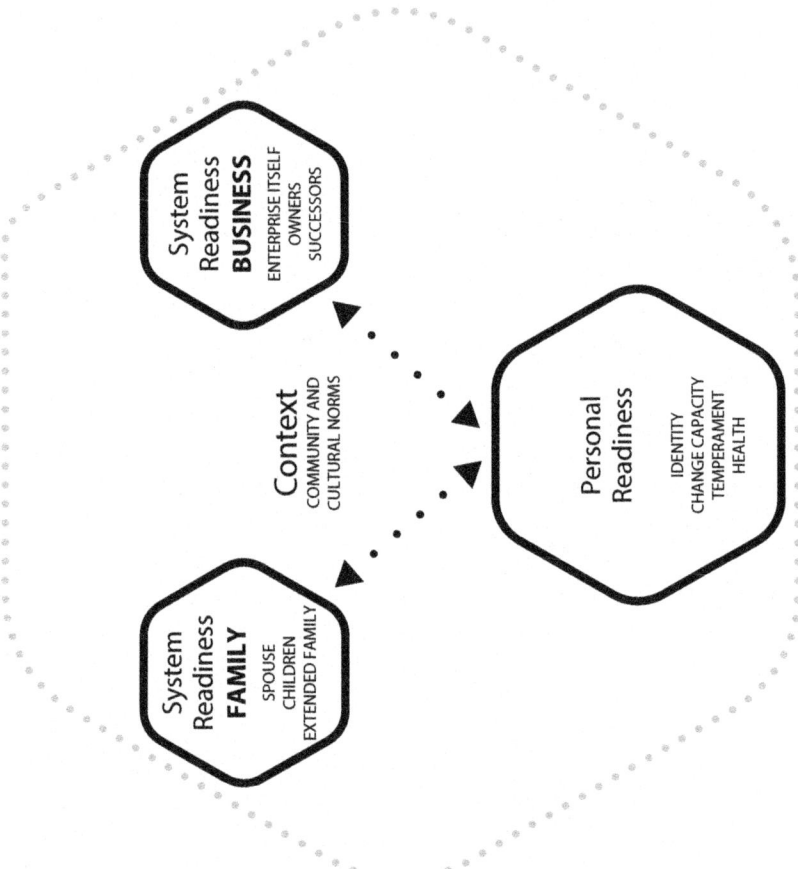

Fig. 7.1 Conceptual model

> We raised three sons and they all still live close to us, we have had 9 of 11 grandchildren in our Sunday school class - so family has been a big, big part of life outside the business.
>
> For 60 years, I have had a hobby of raising trees to give away. I have raised a couple hundred thousand trees in this area from seedlings and that keeps an old man out of trouble.
>
> In addition, I have been on the board of a half a dozen all youth oriented ministries and that has been extremely rewarding. Family and community have always been central to my life, and for that I am deeply grateful.
>
> **JACK HERSCHEND,** RETIRED CEO OF HERSCHEND ENTERTAINMENT

Where You're From

As suggested above, the social/cultural context in which you're making choices and operating will influence your options and experience. Where you come from and live has an impact that is often invisible unless you choose to reflect on it more intentionally and directly. It's like the old adage about the fish being unaware of the water in which it exists; the creature has no frame of reference for a different reality—so the water is "invisible." With that in mind, let's look at the potentially invisible social/cultural factors that will influence your transition.

Is What You Do All of Who You Are?

I grew up in the United States, but my extended family was based in Canada and France, where I traveled often. That gave me an outsider's perspective into American social norms, and I was always struck by how focused those in the United States are on their *professional roles*, even in social settings. In the United States, for example, it's common to be introduced with something like, "This is Stephanie, she's a consultant" or "Meet David, he works in marketing." While I take pride in my professional role, enjoy talking about what I do, and am as guilty as the next person of making just this kind of introduction, I would be less likely to do this in Europe or even some parts of Canada, as that is really not considered polite conversation in social settings of many other countries.

A higher degree of emphasis on the idea that what you do is who you are will most likely create additional pressure around the move to post-work life, because it underlies a pointed question: If you're no longer a professional, who exactly are you? Recall from Chapter 3 the concept of the "identity trap," or allowing just a small number of personal features—mainly what you do for a living—to define you. Certain cultures make falling into that trap more likely, as you'll internalize the norm of emphasis on professional life without even realizing it. Keep that in mind as you think about or undergo the transition.

Consider These Cultural Elements

Beyond the potential identity traps your culture sets (or doesn't set) for you, it's important to consider other key cultural elements that will affect your transition. Broadly, this means thinking about what may be considered "typical" or "appropriate" behavior for successful people of a certain age among your social peers and broader society. Here are some of the key elements to consider, and related questions:

- *Appropriate role of "elders" in the family:* Do senior generation members take an active role in the extended family, whether related to decision-making, providing childcare, or other areas?
- *Appropriate role of "elders" in business:* Do retirees continue to be involved in business areas in an advisory, governance, or other capacity?
- *Willingness to relocate:* Do people tend to move out of the area permanently upon retirement (as is the case for many urban centers), spend a significant part of the year in other locations (as snowbirds do), or stay in their original community long term (the case with many smaller towns)?
- *Nature of travel:* What's the norm for retirement-related travel in your circle of friends? Do people normally travel the country or world, or tend to focus more strongly on local activities—or some combination?
- *Importance of physical activity/athleticism/fitness:* How much does your community and peer group value and provide opportunities for staying fit through a combination of physical activities, healthy eating, and mindfulness exercises?
- *Centrality of volunteering and community service:* What's the norm for getting involved in community-focused activities, such as taking leadership roles in or volunteering with local non-profits, and are there many opportunities for these?
- *Civic/political engagement:* How typical is it for people in post-work stages to become involved in civic matters and/or run for political office?

Naturally, the answers to those queries will vary from community to community, and must be filtered through the interests you've identified as more important to you (more on that in Chapter 8). For example, people in the United States are more likely to move to a warmer location post-retirement than may be the case for other nationals, in part because our culture is highly mobile, individualistic (moving away from extended family, including grandchildren, is not viewed as a big deal), and prioritizes physical comfort.

That said, your *exact location* of residence within the USA also impacts whether you might consider retiring to a new town. As hinted at above, it may be that people who live in smaller towns have a deeper appreciation for local ties and would thus be less likely to move away than someone who worked all their life in a big city—although New Yorkers may take issue with that idea!

> Being in a relatively small town, everybody knows everybody. You don't have to figure out where help is needed - it was easy for me to see where I could plug in.
>
> **JACK HERSCHEND,** RETIRED CEO OF HERSCHEND ENTERTAINMENT

Furthermore, if you come from a more traditional family culture, you may also be disinclined to move, as you will make it a higher priority to stay close to children and grandchildren, even if that means you have to brave sub-zero temperatures or shovel the occasional snow.

Moreover, your willingness to consider living in a new location may also be impacted by the reach of your network. That is, if you have friends and connections who have already made the move to sunny Florida, you may be far more willing to consider that as part of your planning than if you believed your network and opportunities remained anchored largely in your current community. We'll discuss the role of your social network more below, but keep in mind that it may be more important for you to stay close to your primary community if your access to interesting opportunities and rewarding social connections are based mostly there.

The extent of alignment among your home community, personal passions, and network-based opportunities may also have a bearing on what feels possible or desirable as a post-retirement path to fulfillment. For instance, it may be that your community connections open many high-value doors and enable you to extend efforts you had begun around a civic or non-profit project that is deeply rewarding and feels aligned with your core life goals and values. On the other hand, if you feel a strong need or desire to stay close to home but find few opportunities for engagement in your local community, you may need to get creative about shaping these (such as starting a new organization/ initiative) while continuing to meet your needs for family or community closeness. Remember: it's not just the availability of opportunities in general in your local community but also the extent to which they are open to you and would leverage your interests, talents, and experience effectively.

The Experience You Bring

We need to consider your broad base of experience—especially in the professional domain—part of your context as well, because it will have direct bearing on the post-work opportunities available to you. For example, the size, nature, and visibility of the business where you made your career will almost definitely influence the doors that may open for you, and how quickly and widely they do so. If your business is a nationally known brand or one of the larger employers in your community, it is likely that this cachet will create opportunities that may be harder for the retiring leader of a more modest business to access. Retiring leaders from large, well-known firms will generally be solicited more frequently for board service, have better connections to exciting civic engagement, and enjoy other leadership, advisory, and participation opportunities.

Marilyn Carlson Nelson, former Chair and CEO of Carlson, points out how the size and reach of her family firm helped her find post-work opportunities with high-profile organizations.

Today I work with organizations that promote the issues I care most deeply about such as human rights – in particular, the empowerment of women and the protection of children. I continue to advocate for women's engagement more broadly in places like service on the ExxonMobil Board or increased participation at global events like the World Economic Forum in Davos.

I first became interested in protecting children from trafficking when our family foundation co-founded the World Childhood Foundation with the Queen of Sweden in 1999. Today, I am working with several national and local partners in government, business, the NGO community and civil society to combat the exploitation of children.

But there are many ways to work with other high-profile organizations to elevate your own community. As a few examples, in retirement I have worked to entice the NFL to bring Super Bowl LII to Minnesota. I have taught classes to MBA students on the subject of corporate responsibility at the University of Minnesota and I supported the Minnesota Orchestra's accomplishment to be the first professional U.S. orchestra to perform in Cuba since the normalization of relations. Thanks to the platform that grew from our family business, I realized I was in a position to expand my voice and work on these interests - from other very powerful platforms. My passions coupled with business skills and networks have resulted in a highly rewarding momentum for positive change throughout my retirement.

MARILYN CARLSON NELSON, FORMER CHAIR AND CEO OF CARLSON

While not every retiring leader will secure an invite to Davos, or to serve on the board of a major publicly traded firm, or the prestigious Cleveland Clinic hospital or similar organization, most will have access to connections and organizations that may have a long relationship with your company and can lead to compelling opportunities for ongoing engagement.

To consider another aspect of your professional experience, if in the course of your work life you traveled extensively, including overseas, you may have a naturally greater appetite for exposure to other locales and cultures than do those who didn't leave home much. Further, deep experience with travel may give you the confidence and experience you need to pursue leisure travel and opportunities far from home, and even to relish navigating the logistics of time abroad.

Executives who have had less need to travel the globe might either be thrilled by the new opportunity or a little daunted by the challenges that go with that territory. The good news, if you haven't had much global travel experience but are looking forward to these new adventures, is that there is a wealth of travel companies and organizations that can handle all of the logistics and organize a journey from start to finish. Similarly, mobile technology is your friend in this domain, as there are apps for everything from finding the best croissant in Paris to negotiating the London Underground public transportation system—if you're uncomfortable using these, learning them may be easier than you think.

The People in Your Network

Your network plays a large role in your transition, especially as related to opportunities to remain engaged with the world in a meaningful way post-work. As a simple example, consider that a CEO who has not cultivated much of a network beyond their immediate business may struggle to find opportunities that are interesting and stimulating to them post-retirement. On the other hand, even an outgoing leader who has worked to create a social network may not find engaging opportunities if their network doesn't offer relevant or interesting opportunities due to network size, location, or other factors.

Do you have a network of people who represent diverse opportunities for socializing, having fun, traveling, and making professional and community impact in your post-work life? Retiring family business leaders who identify and take advantage of network-based opportunities are much more likely to lead fulfilling and impactful post-retirement lives.

Here we consider this key aspect of your context in more detail.

Value Your Tribe

Humans are naturally communal beings. That is, we need to be part of a "tribe" in some way; it's part of the context for a healthy, fulfilling life. Part of this is for survival: Our prehistoric ancestors didn't last long if they were shunned by their groups and left to fend for themselves for hunting and food collection/preparation. While we no longer rely on tribal membership to sustain life, we still gain multiple benefits from our groups, including an all-important *sense of belonging*.

For most working adults, their professional team fulfills much of their tribal need. Not surprisingly, I've observed that for many business leaders, their professional and social lives are inextricably intertwined: the majority of their socializing is with colleagues from the company, suppliers or vendors, and industry peers (such as through industry associations and conferences). This is partly out of necessity, as business leadership today tends to consume much of one's waking hours and requires a fair amount of working "social" outings, whether a round of golf or a long dinner to "talk shop" or negotiate a deal. Many top executives, then, will develop a strong base of friends who are tied to their work role over the years.

In this sense, business leaders are not unlike professional athletes in team-based sports, who spend so much time with a very close-knit tribe: their team. They work, practice, compete, eat, travel, and stay in hotels or other lodging with their teammates. While business relationships don't always run quite that deep, they are often at the core of a leader's network.

There's nothing inherently wrong with creating a strong work-based social network, and it's to one's benefit on many dimensions to do so. But the challenge is that a sub-set—many, in some cases—of the relationships involved likely won't transcend the professional domain. That is, you may not be able to take your social context with you as easily as you think. That's because shared work was the common interest that served as the basis for the social ties in the first place, leaving little common ground in retirement—if you can't talk about the business, colleagues, or the industry more broadly, there may not be much to talk about at all.

Of course, some work-based relationships run far deeper than the business context in which they emerged, and are thus more likely to survive the leaders' transition into retirement. Even in those cases, however, the *practicalities* of many of the relationships are still contextual—that is, the opportunity to connect is at the annual trade show, or based on being able to grab a quick meal at or near the office. So, when the work-related routines slip away, these social bonds naturally may not be as consistent.

This typical post-retirement decline in social outlets and sense of community can be hard, even though many folks don't necessarily notice the change in a big way or think of it as a loss, especially when it's impending. As these relationships fit into the work context so seamlessly, their importance beyond that world may not be obvious to the retiring leader until it's too late, and they face a post-work life with far fewer social opportunities—adding to the losses from this difficult process. This is especially likely if the leader has done a good job of transitioning and no longer remains deeply connected to the business.

In general, it's important for you to find tribes beyond work to join, gaining fulfillment from spending time with others, directing collective efforts toward some shared purpose. This will come more easily to some people than others. Some of that depends on the type of community in which you live and your experience base, as suggested earlier. But beyond those factors, people with lifelong emphasis on diverse social ties will, not surprisingly, likely enjoy a context with more post-retirement social opportunities, as available through their broader network. Of note, women may have an easier time than men with some aspects of network-building, as the "Women Are More Emotionally Intelligent Than Men (Kind Of)" box suggests.

Women Are More Emotionally Intelligent Than Men (Kind Of)

According to psychologist Daniel Goleman, women have an emotional intelligence advantage over men—to a point.[1] Specifically, women score higher than men on many tests of emotional intelligence, which may help them form more and longer-lasting relationships, including those they can carry into post-retirement life. At the same time, the differences may not be large in many cases, as the gender-based bell curves for the components of emotional intelligence overlap significantly. Similarly, even on core dimensions of emotional intelligence, research finds that women are not stronger than men across the board. For example, while women tend to show superiority on emotional empathy (sensing how others are feeling), men may be inherently (based on brain chemistry) better able to engage in problem-solving related to resolve emotional problems. Neither is necessarily a superior way to approach an emotional issue, but both can lead to the development of meaningful relationships. Interestingly, business leaders at the highest levels have been shown to be similarly high in levels of emotional intelligence, *regardless* of gender. This bodes well for family business leaders looking to make a transition into retirement with support from a strong social network.

As suggested above, temperament will play a large role in the size and nature of your social network (for more on the topic of temperament in general, see Chapter 4 on personal readiness). Despite the strong stereotype of extroverted leaders, plenty of retiring CEOs are quite introverted, and may need to make a more proactive effort to invest in relationship bonds that will protect them from isolation post-work. If you recognize that you may be less likely to reach out naturally to others beyond the professional domain, you may need to take special care to pursue opportunities that fit your interests and enable you to have a healthy balance of social activity and quiet time. Chapter 8 goes into more detail on how to pursue such opportunities.

Understand and Use Your Network's Value

As the material here so far suggests, your network will ideally not be a passive group but a dynamic source of valuable, engaging individuals who may help connect you to new opportunities. Most transitioning executives need others around them who will push them to think and create, share ideas and conquer obstacles together, celebrate victories, and learn from experience and apply that knowledge to future endeavors. This is a natural part of most leaders' DNA, so it's likely part of yours.

That means it's important to develop friendships, mentorships, and other bonds with people who will challenge you, ideally with those who are true *equals* on important dimensions, such that they can inspire and encourage you to continue fulfilling your potential and having real impact. That being said, *diversity* is also a critical network factor; having relationships with a wide range of people—of different ages, from different walks of life, from different cultures and ways of thinking—will typically provide a richer breadth of opportunities and experiences. As we'll discuss in Chapter 8, this can work both ways, especially with younger friends and acquaintances, such that you may guide them as a mentor, while learning and taking inspiration from their youth and ideas. In fact, research suggests that gaining younger friends in later stages of life enhances one's life more than would additional retirement income.[2]

In general, longtime friends and collaborators are core to your network, and can help you stay engaged with life, whether through enjoying a round of golf, sharing a thought-provoking conversation over dinner, or joining forces to take on a new professional, non-profit, or civic/political challenge.

For example, a recently retired family business leader I know was part of a "mini board of directors," a group of retired professionals who had all enjoyed successful business careers, some in family business, some in non-family firms. When my acquaintance had an idea for a new business venture, they encouraged him to explore it fully and helped him do that in earnest, rolling up their sleeves to flesh out the idea and help him with its early stages by providing insights, contacts, and encouragement.

Similarly, by joining new groups and efforts—whether discovered through your network or not—you may broaden your social ties and find valuable, enriching new contacts, as Frank Schurz, former CEO of Schurz Communication, did through his board service. "The friendship you form on these boards is remarkable," he explains. "You walk in as a stranger and then next thing you know the room is filled with your ten best friends. Getting to know them and their families is always fascinating."

Society's Broader Norms

Earlier in this chapter, we talked about how the social norms of your peer group, local community, city, state, or region will influence your transition to post-work life. This is also true of the broader society in which you live, at the level of country.

Take perceptions of age, for example. In Chapter 4, we acknowledged that your physical health and vitality will have an impact on the opportunities you can or want to pursue as you transition away from business leadership: In general, the healthier you are, the broader the range of activities you can pursue across domains. However, even if you are in great health, perceptions of age in our culture can play a role in your experience of this transition and the number and nature of opportunities available to you.

> I was told I'd be a good director - but most people want an active CEO and I'm retired and 74 years old. We wouldn't have invited a director that age for our board, either.
>
> **MURRAY BERSTEIN,** FOUNDER AND FORMER CEO OF NIXON UNIFORM SERVICE & MEDICAL WEAR

This is unfortunate, because while there is clear value in leaders transitioning out of the day-to-day operations of their business—which enables new ideas and talents to flourish and take the enterprise to the next stage—it can be a monumental loss when retiring executives who still have tremendous ideas, insights, and energy are simply "put out to pasture" due to lack of imagination on how to leverage the talents they can bring to many situations. This trend is fueled by factors such as age limits for board service (a limit of 70, for example, may be unnecessarily arbitrary in a society where people maintain vitality well beyond that age), the biased assumptions that older adults have less energy or are out of touch, or the inability to conceive of key roles in a part-time model. These and other realities may impede retiring executives from fulfilling their potential and organizations from realizing the benefit of such individuals' experience and insight.

In this context, it's clear that just as the senior generation needs to "get out of the way" of the next generation to enable them to grow, learn, and lead, the younger generation needs to find ways to engage with the senior generation, or "make room for their elders," such that their wisdom and perspective is available for the good of organizations throughout society.

The "Combat Ageism!" box offers tips for ensuring you continue to stay engaged with your broad community in mutually beneficial ways (Table 7.1).

Table 7.1: Combat Ageism!

Here are several interrelated ways to prevent age from impeding your engagement with and contributions to your community:

- *Adopt an engagement mindset:* Do your best to find opportunities and stay engaged – in the discussion, in your industry, in your community. The more you remain active, visible, and 'relevant' the more people will enjoy being with you and seek your advice and perspective.

- *Don't try to beat them, join them:* Surround yourself with younger people by embracing opportunities to learn from the rising generation as you share your wisdom and experience with them as well (see the next chapter for specific ideas on how to do this).

- *Stay fit:* Physical health and high energy are powerful markers of vitality that not only enable you to 'keep up' with your board peers, other collaborators, grandchildren, and tennis partners, but also send a powerful signal that you still have plenty to contribute and the energy with which to contribute it.

- *Get out:* Stay connected with your network and continue to expand that network.

Your Work Set-up

Yes, most retired people still have a work set-up, as paradoxical as that may sound. Work is where most of us go the majority of days, regardless of what that means: a corporate office, a home office, a client site, or wherever. So, your work set-up will be a large part of the transition to post-work life. Moving out of a traditional work set-up into a home office or no office at all is challenging, no matter how much you may be looking forward to it. We humans struggle with change, especially one this large.

> One thing you really miss is the staff - the small things that used to be done. Now you have to become the clerk. You are going to have to create a new safety net... you get to a certain point where some of this administrative stuff is more of a grind.
>
> **FRANK SCHURZ,** FORMER CEO OF SCHURZ COMMUNICATION

To navigate the transition in work set-up, think about how to handle these key areas:

- *Where:* Where will you work, whether on your new business ventures/ideas, non-profit or civic leadership or advisory role, painting, poetry, or any other pursuit? Your original office, a different one, your home, some combination? Is this an ideal location for you, given your past experience with productivity? (Be careful with retaining your original work office or another within the family firm headquarters, as this may complicate the leadership transition. A good compromise is to work in the family office, if your enterprise has one, or a satellite office, to stay near but far.)
- *Who:* Who, if anyone, will you retain for any kind of administrative support, such as a part-time executive assistant? Will you be collaborating regularly with anyone, including mentors or mentees? If yes to any of these, where will you meet? Remember, retired leaders often struggle with the loss of administrative support, in part because they underestimate how much their assistants did for them, from planning travel to paying bills to answering phones. So, think hard about the tasks that

would be best to outsource to someone, and the logistics of such collaboration: whom to hire, where to have them work, how much they will work, how much you will pay them, and others.
- *How:* Beyond the question of administrative support above, how will you manage administrative issues, including schedule management, correspondence, personal finances, transportation, travel logistics, and others? What about files? Many CEOs remain involved at a board level or other, and new projects or interests may generate papers and documents that must be managed effectively. So, with that in mind, what kind of desk, computer, and printer set-up do you need? Are you sufficiently tech-savvy and comfortable to work mostly on a screen, or do you like to look at hard copies?
- *When:* When will you work? Will you keep business/office hours or work on a more flexible schedule? What will your typical daily, weekly, and monthly routine look like? How well does this suit your personality and habits? How will this routine impact your spouse or others?
- *What:* Given your answers to the questions above, what's realistic in terms of finances? What compromises must you make, if any?

Your work set-up may depend in part on whether you still have responsibilities related to the enterprise. For example, Phil Clemens, former CEO of the Clemens Family Corporation, was asked by the company's board to continue teaching the leadership class he'd helped establish. He agreed to take an office away from the executive suite, along with a budget to cover some of his travel in a separate role as family ambassador. Striking the right balance between what is practical to meet your needs, while respecting boundaries takes real thought and planning, and can make a positive difference in your transition.

Notes

1. Material in the box based on Daniel Goleman, "Are Women More Emotionally Intelligent Than Men?" *Psychology Today*, April 29, 2011, https://www.psychologytoday.com/blog/the-brain-and-emotional-intelligence/201104/are-women-more-emotionally-intelligent-men (accessed February 20, 2017).
2. As cited in George Vaillant, *Aging Well* (Little, Brown and Co., Boston, 2002).

8

Where Do You Want to Go (and How Do You Know?)

> You have to think about your life after work. It isn't just going to happen.
>
> **FRANK SCHURZ,** FORMER CEO OF SCHURZ COMMUNICATION

"I was clear on what I wanted to do in retirement," says Jack Herschend, former CEO of Herschend Entertainment, "I just didn't realize all the other opportunities that were out there." He goes on to list the areas he planned to explore in post-work life: serving in the ministry, mentoring young business leaders and others, being involved in his grandchildren's lives, being a "cheerleader" for—rather than a critic of—his family business, and pursuing a hobby that benefited others. Among the specific things he's done have been donating trees he raised himself to residents of areas hit by tornadoes, and writing about 25 notes per week to the family business employees about good things he sees them doing.

Herschend's story suggests we've come to an important juncture in the journey that this book represents: helping you develop your personal continuity plan.

Hopefully, by now you have read about many ideas and insights that will support your personal transition from your leadership role, including how to assess and think about your personal readiness and that of the business and family from which you come, along with the broader context in which all of these systems exist: the cultural, social (network), and physical environments (including work set-up).

The broad goal, of course, is to make the next phase and steps in your transition as fulfilling as possible. In that context, the specific aim of this chapter is to help you:

- Be aware of the "whys" that drive you at a basic level;
- Think through the range and balance of opportunities you may consider post-work;
- Understand yourself and what will be more appealing to you from the many choices available (self-assessment);
- Engage in concrete planning for next steps.

In short, in the major sections below, we'll explore *where* you may want to go, and *how* you can know that. But first let's consider the bigger picture of *why* it may be important to stay busy in this phase of life in the first place.

Think About Your Why

Why stay busy in retirement?

It's a good question for anyone, especially those who have been immersed full-time in interesting, demanding, often all-consuming work, as most senior family business leaders would have been. On one hand, as retirement nears it may be tempting to want to do *nothing* but relax, check in on the business occasionally, and enjoy time and travel with family and friends. After all, you may feel that you've been working hard for the majority of your waking hours for decades (you probably have been). But for most family business executives, the "do nothing" post-work recipe is inadequate.

> CEOs have a lot to contribute and give. Your next chapter should *never* be inactivity. Be guided by your passions to make a difference in the world. Mentor others, serve on boards, pursue philanthropy. CEOs come with capabilities needed in so many places.
>
> **DICK DEVOS,** FORMER PRESIDENT OF AMWAY

Why Most Leaders Must Stay Active in Retirement

The crux of it is that a person with a strong internal drive—a fair characterization for the vast majority of family enterprise leaders—needs productive outlets through which to channel that drive. There are two significant motivators at play here. First, transitioning into retirement inevitably involves a *sense of loss*, as we alluded to in our discussion of the "identity trap" that suggests much of who we are, including our perception of core self, is what we do professionally. It's natural to want to diminish that feeling, to take back some sense of control over both the big picture and the day-to-day of your life.

"I don't want to become invisible, or to become a burden," I've heard many transitioning family enterprise leaders say when they're being completely honest. Eric Allyn, former co-chair of Welch Allyn, remarks, "I always knew what my objectives were when I was in the business. I thought of myself as an employee more than as an owner, so losing that identity, objectives, and structure was hard." This natural fear of irrelevance and unstructured time is important to acknowledge and, more importantly, to use as motivation to seek out new ways to be relevant post-work.

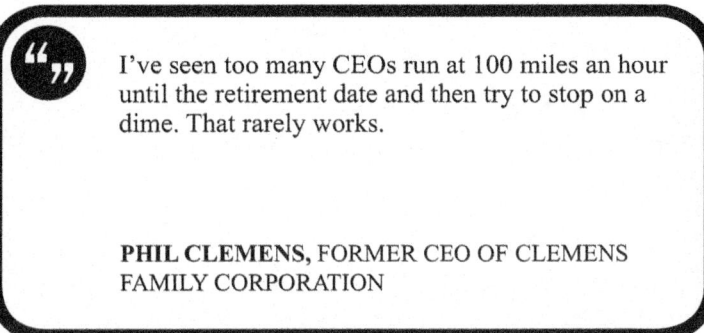

I've seen too many CEOs run at 100 miles an hour until the retirement date and then try to stop on a dime. That rarely works.

PHIL CLEMENS, FORMER CEO OF CLEMENS FAMILY CORPORATION

Second, and more positively, the *need to have an impact* is profound for many of us, especially more ambitious people such as long-serving business leaders. Innovation icon Steve Jobs famously said, "We're here to put a dent in the universe," and he certainly lived by that principle.[1] This dent-making is what drives many leaders across sectors. During their primary career, their leadership of an enterprise enables them to fulfill that ambition on multiple dimensions: their company can make an impact on how people live through its products and services; the vision and strategy they create and the operations they oversee may improve the economics of their shareholders, employees, and the broader community; their guidance may impact the career path and decisions of many on their team; and so on.

It is this specific drive for impact that makes me worry about a CEO who tells me their retirement plans revolve around "golf and travel." No matter how much you enjoy golf and travel, unless you are organizing an annual charity golf event or engaged in large-scale service tourism, you may not feel you are impacting much with these pursuits, even if you meaningfully improve your golf handicap!

> I measure meaning and satisfaction by three metrics: relationships, continuing to grow and learn and be engaged, and leaving a legacy.
>
> **DAVID GELLER,** CO-FOUNDER AND CEO OF JOYN (FORMERLY GV FINANCIAL)

In order to evaluate the importance of impact to you in your planning for this next phase of life, you may find it informative to take the assessment in Table 8.1, and to reflect on what the scoring guide (found in Appendix 3) suggests may be true for you.

In addition to considering how important it might be to you to be involved in activities that "make an impact"—you may also want to reflect on the importance of scale to you on this. That is, some individuals strive to make an impact that touches a wide range of people or processes. For example, they may work to invent a process that significantly improves how something is made in their industry, or finance a parenting training class for high-risk parents that will impact hundreds of families in their community. Others are more focused on a deeper and more directly tangible impact: mentoring a young executive who has great potential but is really struggling, or financing a refugee family from their church to help get them on their feet—to include housing, clothing, food, and job search support. Obviously, these are all powerful ways to make a difference in the world; my point is merely to observe what has motivated you over the years and use that insight to help you think about where and how you'd like to pursue impact in your post-career stage of life.

Table 8.1: Importance of Impact

Please indicate, on a scale of 1 to 4 the extent to which you agree with the following statements...

Not at all	A little	Somewhat	A lot
1	2	3	4

Statement	1	2	3	4
I want to be at the forefront of new ideas or involved with substantive innovation…	☐	☐	☐	☐
I want my actions or decisions to change a lot of lives…	☐	☐	☐	☐
It is important to me that my ideas influence others…	☐	☐	☐	☐
I want to leave a legacy	☐	☐	☐	☐
It is important to me that my ideas are adopted	☐	☐	☐	☐
It is important to me that I can see the results of my efforts…	☐	☐	☐	☐
It is important to me that my life will have made a big difference to others…	☐	☐	☐	☐
SUM of POINTS: _____				

The Challenge of Engagement

The importance of staying active in a fulfilling way means you have to find ways to be productively engaged once you are no longer in a business leadership role. And that can be challenging for many. While engagement in business leadership is tied to bottom-line results and business development goals, post-work life doesn't naturally have as many inherent opportunities for tangible impact. Thus, access to projects, especially compelling ones, requires active pursuit of rewarding opportunities. You may seek out such opportunities largely on your own, but many can be developed through your personal connections—not just social connections with whom to travel, play golf, or dine, as discussed earlier—but those who can serve as conduits, recommenders, and sounding boards regarding new ideas and opportunities.

The next section helps you think about where you want to go, in terms of the activities that will make up your post-work life.

Where Do You Want to Go?

Whether leading a non-profit board, starting a new business venture, spearheading a church fundraiser, or cultivating a garden club, staying active enables former business leaders to find fulfillment on multiple dimensions. The active pursuit of interests enables a person to maintain connections, grow and strive toward important and rewarding goals, and develop a community of collaborators and friends.

So, what do you want to do?

It's good first to understand the universe of possible activities you can take on, and then to think about which fit you best, based on your personality and interests. Depending on where you are in the transition, your "dance card" may be quite full already with post-work opportunities, or you may be just beginning to think about what's next. Either way, consider new or larger-scale opportunities in the categories below. The goal isn't to find the one thing that will make you happy but to approach the activities of post-work life as a *portfolio* that, taken together, will keep you engaged, satisfied, and fulfilled.[2] More on this in Chapter 9.

Leadership

Professional and Non-profit Leadership

As part of planning for his eventual retirement from Robbie Fantastic Flexibles, Irv Robinson and a group of friends started a non-profit to provide internships at non-profits for college students. "We're mentors to these kids during the summer and they learn how to write grants, and then we have them go through their presentations and we actually give grants from my family's philanthropic initiatives to help at-risk kids," Irv explains. "I have had a complete ball doing this. I love the opportunity to create and make a difference."

Perhaps the easiest transition for retiring leaders to make is, not surprisingly, toward new leadership, management, or advisory roles—familiar territory for family business executives. Under the broad umbrella of leadership, it may be easiest to focus on professional roles, such as pursuit of new business ventures, trade association leadership, or corporate board directorships, again because these are similar to the work you've been doing for years.

But not every retiring CEO is able (or wants) to serve on a board, start another business, or otherwise remain deeply entrenched in the traditional work world. The good news is that many opportunities for leadership exist among non-profits, including social impact and religious organizations, that would benefit deeply from your skills/knowledge. For example, consider your local house of worship, food bank, or chapter of YMCA or Goodwill. Many of these are large, complex organizations in their own right, with significant staffs, budgets, and goals. Another great example might be your local community college or university—these may need new members for their board of trustees, feature an innovation lab for which they need guidance, or offer opportunities for you to be a visiting instructor or "entrepreneur in residence" to share your experience and wisdom with students and faculty.

High schools, too, can benefit from your skills and insights. Murray Berstein, founder and former CEO of Nixon Uniform Service and Medical Wear, has been involved with a local high school for about ten years:

When I learned that 30% of students don't graduate high school I became very motivated. I got involved with the school near my plant and we put together a 'board of advisors' for the school that focused on how we could get more kids to graduate. It didn't take us long to figure out what they needed. A lot of kids drop out of school because of dysfunction at home. We got involved trying to increase the number of advisors who could work with these kids.

MURRAY BERSTEIN, FOUNDER AND FORMER CEO OF NIXON UNIFORM SERVICE AND MEDICAL WEAR

As Murray's story suggests, "leadership" needn't mean running the entire place, nor will that opportunity necessarily be available to you. As suggested above, you may well pursue the highest level of leadership, but it would also be good to explore the possibility of running a specific project or initiative (such as fundraising), acting in an advisory role (whether solo or as part of an advisory board/group), serving as a trustee, or others.

Especially if you're aiming for a leadership role of any kind, choose your target organizations carefully. The specific type of *impact* it has will be particularly important, as previewed earlier; that means the *purpose, vision, and mission* should resonate with you, and you should have some conviction that the organization is effective in achieving these (or will be with your help), as we'll discuss more subsequently in this chapter. If there are multiple organizations that fit this bill, it may make sense to ramp up your time and energy with one with which you already have *existing ties or involvement*. What better organization to seek to enrich than one to which you've already devoted time, energy, or financial sponsorship?

An example of the pursuit of such natural offshoots of existing activities would be a transitioning leader who takes on a formal role with their church or synagogue after being involved informally for decades; they've donated to the organization and volunteered for narrow roles in the past but now may be able to increase the scale and depth of their participation by chairing a major fundraising campaign.

Furthermore, while many organizations may be eager to benefit from what you bring to the table, not all of them will be *structured* in a way that suits your style or interests, in terms of organizational chart, processes for strategic and operational planning, and financial structure/management. Like any possible project or opportunity, it's important to engage in good due diligence on fit, for mutual benefit.

It's also important not to over-commit to a given leadership activity or set of these. Phil Clemens, former CEO of the Clemens Family Corporation, for example, commits up to 10% of his time to non-profit boards, and pledges to be on a board only for three years, after which he decides if his director role continues to be mutually beneficial. If he's asked to join a new board, he'll often ask the organization to wait until he finishes an existing directorship tenure.

Saying no to people is hard, especially when you have real relationships with them. What works for me is to get clear on why I would do it or why I wouldn't and then just communicate that. Transparency tends to work for me.

IRV ROBINSON, CO-FOUNDER AND FORMER CEO OF ROBBIE FANTASTIC FLEXIBLES

Finally, note an important leadership-related caveat. Some transitioning leaders make the mistake of assuming their reputation and experience is sufficient in and of itself to attract new opportunities for professional or community leadership, with minimal effort on their part. In reality, that may not be the case. In fact, if you have a strong reputation or standing in the community based on business leadership, people may actually be apprehensive about approaching you for help, seeing you as a caricature or making false assumptions about your interest or intent. The points that follow suggest a few reasons people may be reluctant to invite you to specific opportunities:

- *Inferiority*: "They're used to dealing with much bigger, more important issues, so they would never be willing to help us."
- *Fear of takeover*: "If they join us they would try to take charge of everything."
- *Intimidation*: "They would think we're not smart enough or experienced enough to collaborate with."

This will begin to sound like a broken record, but that's why *relationships* are critical for connecting with rewarding post-work opportunities in professional or community domains. If you're a known quantity in a social network, people will be much more likely to understand how you might fit into their organizations or activities. By that same token, the more diverse your experience, the more and wider-ranging opportunities you'll have exposure to and be able to take advantage of through your social ties. A large, rich network simply makes it easier to fill the calendar of post-work life.

Arts and Cultural Activities

In the later stages of their careers, many transitioning leaders haven't had the time or space to get as deeply involved in arts and cultural activities as they would have liked, whether pursuing artistry itself—painting, writing, photography, music, or any other—or helping to lead/govern an arts-focused or cultural organization, such as a museum or ethnicity-based community organization. Now's your chance.

Naturally, some of these opportunities would be covered by the non-profit leadership ideas detailed above, but I wanted to call out arts and culture in a separate section because many former or soon-to-be-former leaders might discount or dismiss these domains. That's a mistake, so don't rule out possibilities for leading arts-focused efforts or taking on a creative pursuit. I've seen many former family business leaders find a real passion for art, often one they never realized they had. Forty-third US president George W. Bush didn't realize how much interest he had in painting for most of his life, and even kept his pursuit of the hobby secret from others, ultimately "outing" himself only after a hacker gained access to digital images of his work and posted several.[3] The ex-president talks about how painting keeps him active and relaxed at the same time. So, don't overlook opportunities for involvement in the arts or culture.

Civic/Political Opportunities

Another category of opportunities that may not be top of mind is the civic/political domain. Do you have passion for influencing local, state, or national issues such as education, healthcare, or infrastructure? Are you excited by the possibility of being involved in government or civic activities at one of these levels? Again, the range of ways to take part in such activities varies widely, with possibilities including school and public library board work, city/municipality positions (such as alderperson or mayor), state-level roles such as commissioners of various areas, and of course federal-level offices including senator and representative. Several of the retired CEOs with whom I spoke had taken an active role in civic matters, from local community leadership roles to running for state-wide office.

There are long-standing ties between business and political leadership for good reason, given the overlap in many of the responsibilities: setting vision and strategy, motivating large numbers of people to believe in you and your ideas, managing crises, communicating articulately to crowds. That said, civic and political engagement is not for everybody, and to do it well requires ongoing passion and a willingness to "play a game" that may involve multiple personal and professional trade-offs. For example, if you are the kind of leader who thrives on building consensus and strives for near-unanimous agreement, government work may be more challenging for you than for others less focused on satisfying all constituents all the time.

Questions to Help You Choose Among Roles

So far, I've focused on the need to do *something* beyond rest and leisure activities in your post-work life. But of course, there's the possibility that you'll take on too much—driven leader types tend to say "yes" too often.

With that in mind, below is a long list of questions you can ask about organizations in which you may consider involving yourself. You don't have to ask all of them, and you don't even have to be bound by the answers. But keeping them in mind, along with what you learn in the later section about "How do you know?", will help you devote your efforts and energy to the right opportunities for you.

- *Mission*: Is the organization's mission aligned with your values? Why or why not?
- *People*: Do you know people there well and have you worked with them before? Is this a team of people you will respect and who will put in the kind of effort that fits your own work style? Are there new collaborators there with whom you're excited about working?
- *Synergy*: Are your skills and experience likely to be valued by the organization? If yes, why?
- *Your goals*: What are you looking to accomplish through your involvement? Is the organization likely to be receptive to your ideas and goals—or do you risk being too much of a disrupter (unintentionally doing more harm than good)?
- *Experience*: Do you have experience with the organization already, or with its general mission and activities in any capacity?
- *Shared leadership (or subordination)*: You likely won't be the top leader—is that okay, or do you need to find a project or opportunity where you can be in charge or a fairly autonomous leader?
- *Collaboration:* Will you be able to work with the full-time team that is there now? Will they be able to work with you?
- *Partnership*: Do you want to partner with someone on this project or effort? Who would be the best candidate(s)?
- *Time*: How much time are you willing to commit, realistically? Is this enough to have real impact? Will the organization expect you to contribute more time than you wish to?
- *Metrics*: Does the organization have clear measures for its performance/success? How will you know if you are succeeding on important dimensions? (see more on this in Chapter 9).
- *Money*: Are you willing to put financial resources into this effort? How much?
- *Excitement*: Based on your answers to everything above, how excited and passionate do you feel about this opportunity?

Play

Much of this book is built on the premise that "play" alone won't satisfy you fully in retirement. Here we consider the other side: that you won't feel fulfilled *unless* you also identify leisure activities that you enjoy, and make these also part of your post-work life. "The challenge in retirement is to combine the fruits of maturity with the recovery of childlike wonder," argues researcher George Vaillant.[4] Playful pursuits are critical for a sense of joy and engagement for all of us.

Playful Pursuits

There are practically as many fun activities as there are people, but here are some significant major categories, with examples:

- *Sports and fitness*: Golf, tennis, racquetball, softball, sailing, running, swimming, rock-climbing, skydiving, weight lifting, bocce ball;
- *Brain games (solo or group-based)*: Card games (bridge, poker, solitaire, and others), Scrabble, Sudoku, Mah-jongg, crossword puzzles, math/logic-based brain teasers;
- *Art-based hobbies*: Painting, drawing, music, acting/improvisation, reading, writing, knitting, crochet;
- *Outings (social or individual)*: Dinners, movies, symphonies, concerts, stage plays, poetry/fiction readings, talks/presentations;
- *Travel (official tours or do-it-yourself)*: local, regional, national, global.

Now, theoretically, you have or will have more time for such pursuits than ever before in your adult life. You don't need to be a cliff-diving adrenaline junkie or a world-class Scrabble player to find enjoyment in playful pursuits. The main idea is to think about what you enjoy most among the categories above or others and how you can fit target activities into any other obligations such as family commitments, leadership, or volunteer responsibilities.

Make It Social

Of course, many such fun activities may be pursued alone—although tennis could be a difficult solo pursuit!—but they tend to be more enriching when enjoyed with others. Spending time on hobbies or mutual interests with others not only makes the activities more rewarding in the moment but also creates shared memories that provide a greater sense of meaning throughout life. In their twilight years, many people look to the past as the "good times," with a sense of wistfulness and loss. That implies that there aren't many meaningful times ahead, which would naturally be discouraging. Making it a point to spend quality time with others, whether hiking Machu Picchu, going on an African safari, competing in a tennis doubles tournament, or merely enjoying quiet time to catch up with a friend over lunch or coffee, social activities give you more things to look forward to, however small. So, think about who and how many among your network—spouse, broader family, friends—will help you enjoy social playtime, and consider branching out if you don't see many options.

In line with this idea, travel is considered a hallmark of retired life, with seniors representing a large contingent of tour groups, cruises, and DIY tourists. Here again, there's no reason travel can't be a solitary pursuit. But the point made above remains: such activities are often more enjoyable and create more meaningful shared memories when they occur with family or in groups.

Finding travel-mates among friends and family can be tricky, given the wide range of compromises a group journey represents as related to activities to pursue, eating and sleeping arrangements, daily schedule, and other things. But again, the effort can be well worth it, as building a social dimension into travel makes for the sharing of multiple viewpoints, more interesting conversation and insights, and even pooling of energy, such that responsibility for forging through difficult times—for instance, airport delays or long hikes—falls on a greater number of shoulders.

Travel is a vehicle through which many needs and relationships can be nurtured. From a getaway to reconnect with your spouse, to an opportunity to visit with old industry friends to maintain those connections, to exploring new interests (e.g., tour to further your knowledge of architecture) or nurturing old ones (e.g., leading a youth mission trip), to a vehicle for bringing your family together—travel opens doors and creates or strengthens connections. While getting budgets and calendars aligned can certainly make travel planning complex, committing to getting out there to explore the world with friends and family is deeply enriching.

Enrichment

All of the pursuits we've covered so far—professional and community leadership and play activities—may be considered enriching on multiple dimensions. But in this last category we consider activities you may take on to *learn* new things just for yourself, now that you have more time to explore long-dormant or newly discovered interests. Naturally, some learning goals will be aimed at supporting other passions, pursuits, and roles—for example, taking up a language to facilitate travel or a board governance workshop to strengthen one's ability to contribute as a director.

In other cases, you may see the activity as a new "proving ground" for you in any number of areas: physical or artistic capability, discipline, persistence, and so on. Again, the goal needn't be to become an expert or world-class competitor (but if that's what you want to do, go for it!). Rather it's about developing yourself in a new area that may be fulfilling on one or more dimensions.

>  Get out of your head… Get out of your comfort zone. Expose yourself to real-world challenges.
>
> **DAVID JUDAY,** FORMER CEO OF IDEAL INDUSTRIES

As suggested in the previous section, these may be pursuits that can be taken up individually (but likely in a group setting, such as a writing class), with your life partner, or with a group of friends. Incorporating a social element can make the enrichment activity more enjoyable, while keeping you committed, as you can share your goals with others and be inspired by their goals and progress.

Below are some categories of enrichment activities people are likely to pursue in retirement, with examples (these overlap naturally with some of the activities noted in previous sections):

- *Classes, workshops, seminars*: Language, arts, architecture, technology (programming, social media), governance, leadership;
- *Clubs*: Book clubs, sports-related clubs, travel clubs, arts clubs, garden clubs, movie clubs;
- *Teaching*: Language, arts, technology, business, leadership, governance, writing (consider stretching yourself by teaching a class on a subject for which you're not an "expert");
- *Spirituality*: Prayer/discussion groups, mentorship by a spiritual leader, spiritual pilgrimage.

How Do You Know?

"Good decisions take time," says Peter Buffet, son of Warren Buffett and a successful musician and author in his own right. "They are processes, not spasms, they call for self-knowledge; and self-knowledge—like it or not—calls for a certain amount of gut-checking."[5]

How do you know which post-work opportunities are the right ones to pursue?

As importantly, how do you avoid pursuing the wrong opportunities—or too many opportunities altogether?

Even though I'm only in my late 40s as I write this, I definitely find myself saying things like "I'm too old for this nonsense" more often in response to things that don't seem worth my time or attention. I've outgrown many things, and have much better perspective than I did even five years ago about where best to direct my energy and resources.

My point is that it's important for you to find the pursuits that truly fit your personality, interests, and goals. Rare is the person who becomes more flexible and adaptable as they age, so your self-awareness with regard to what you want to do is paramount, for your own well-being and those of the systems of which you are a part. For example, you may not enjoy working with an organization where everyone else is decades younger than you; or maybe that suits you. Best to take some inventory of yourself before committing to specific pursuits. This section will help you do that.

> Take some time - maybe 3 to 6 months - to reflect on what you want. Give yourself time to settle emotionally, discern your real passions - the quiet is important to get clarity.
>
> **DICK DEVOS,** FORMER PRESIDENT OF AMWAY

Identify Your Core Passions

You may have many talents and a broad base of experience on which to draw, but what are you *most* passionate about? In this stage of life, you can pursue your interests with an unprecedented combination of time, mental space, and resources. So, consider the broad, non-mutually exclusive domains where you can direct your passions.

One way to do this is through the "Individual Drivers Exercise" in Table 8.2, which gets at your core motivations (drivers), to guide you toward the activities and areas that will be most fulfilling.[6]

Now, using what you learned from the exercise in Table 8.2, think about the type of pursuits that are well suited to your core drivers. The way you allocate your 100 points can help to clarify the sorts of post-leadership opportunities you want to pursue, and where you may want to focus more of your time. The goal is to help you reflect on activities that you will find intrinsically rewarding. Consider the following list of activities drawn from the themes revealed in my interviews and other sources—these are not exhaustive by any means, they are meant only to inspire thinking and ideas you could develop for yourself:

- *Leading or advising business efforts*: Entrepreneurship, joint ventures, private equity, angel investing;
- *Developing and exploring new or old passions*: Travel, sailing, cycling, art;
- *Developing others*: Mentoring (see more below), coaching, teaching, team-building;
- *Committing time to family*: Expanding role with grandchildren, family travel;
- *Governing organizations or constituents*: Board service in the private and non-profit sectors, public office;
- *Giving back*: Leading or contributing to a non-profit or fundraising effort.

You can work to understand which of these—it can of course be more than one—resonates most with you in two ways. First, without over-thinking, scan the list and see which ones seem most appealing to you at a gut level, along with trying to identify any others that may not be on the list. Second, take a more deliberate approach, thinking back on your journey so far and looking for "bright spots," or the times you really lost yourself in a given activity or pursuit, regardless of the job description of which it was part, or the specific goal or outcome involved. Psychologists call this kind of immersion "flow," and it is associated with great performance and fulfillment.[7] So it's important to find the types of activities that are more likely to place you into "flow" mode, and look to build these into your post business leadership life.

 **Table 8.2: Individual Drivers**

When it comes to any activity we may pursue, we are all motivated by different things. Please rank the following common motivators (or "drivers") in terms of importance to you by distributing a total of 100 points among those items that are your most important motivators.

The item that is the greatest motivator to you will have the most points associated with it. For example, if you are mostly driven to help others, then "Altruism" would receive more points than any other item. Please spread your 100 points among a minimum of three drivers.

It's okay to have some drivers with 0 points (which would mean that those items do not matter to you at all). Try to be as honest with yourself as possible – there are no 'better' drivers than others. Get input from people who know you well if you feel their insights will help.

Driver	Description	Points (Total to 100)
Recognition	Appreciate attention, visibility, approval, and praise	
Control	Desire for success, accomplishment, status, and control	
Fun	Orientation for fun, pleasure, and enjoyment	
Altruism	Desire to help others and contribute to society	
Affiliation	Desire for and enjoyment of social interaction and strong people connections	
Tradition	Dedication, strong personal beliefs, attachment to culture and norms	
Security	Need for predictability, structure, and order	
Commerce	Interest in money, profits, investment, and business opportunities	
Aesthetics	Need for self-expression, concern over look, feel, and design	
Science	Quest for knowledge, research, technology, and data	
	Total	100

Exercise adapted from Hogan, R., & Hogan, J. (2007). Hogan Personality Inventory manual (3rd ed.). Tulsa, OK: Hogan Assessment Systems.

Filter Using Your Personal Criteria

Next, use what you learn from the thought exercises above to identify the general types of activities most fulfilling for you, then filter these activities further by thinking through what you prefer with regard to the criteria that follow. Feel free to add any other criteria you may consider to be important; this is by no means an exhaustive list, it is again meant to stimulate your thinking about the nature of the activity and experiences you will find more rewarding. When you consider HOW that work or activity is pursued, which of these descriptors would reflect the right fit for your style and preferences?

- *Collaboration*: Working on projects or activities, with others versus working alone;
- *Age group*: The need to be with same-age peers, younger individuals, or a mix;
- *Meaning/purpose*: Whether the effort is directed toward some greater good;
- *Structure*: How structured are the work and its setting;
- *Time frame*: How short or long term the effort is expected to be;
- *Measurability*: Whether the outcome of the activity may be measured, and how.

Choose and Test Opportunities

The final step involves going back to the earlier sections of this chapter to consider the universe of possible opportunities—business/community leadership, arts, civic/political engagement, and play—and using what you learned about yourself in this section to decide what makes the shortlist, or what is the right amount of time you would devote in your portfolio to that specific effort. Then learn more about concrete opportunities available, "test" these out as you can (attending an event, sitting in on a meeting as an observer/ad hoc advisor, or going to an introductory class) to gain more evidence of fit.

As much as we talk about planning, and as critical as this may feel for you, it's important to start *doing* something as part of your post-work life as well. Aim for a healthy balance of thinking and acting, as this will help inform your way forward.

Is Mentorship Right for You?

I've devoted this last section to mentorship, a popular activity for many retired family business leaders but again one where a thoughtful, strategic approach will yield the most fulfilling outcomes for all parties.

Sharing your wisdom and experience to guide rising leaders or other professionals can be a highly rewarding activity. But it may not be for everyone. In order to develop meaningful and rewarding roles for your life post-career, you need to be honest with yourself about where you can add value and reap fulfillment, including with regard to mentorship.

The most effective mentors are patient, communicative, and able to place themselves in the shoes of others. Mentors add real value when they are willing to commit regular time to the relationship and be proactive about their guidance but are not so directive that they "micromanage" their mentee or do their work for them. Importantly, if it's a natural role for you, an interest in mentorship will likely be present well before you retire: you will have been a formal or informal mentor already, whether in the professional or community domain.

As with the exercises earlier in the chapter, think through the dimensions of mentorship and what might fit you best:

> Mentoring is a huge, huge opportunity that is available to most all of us.
>
> **JACK HERSCHEND,** FORMER CEO, HERSCHEND ENTERTAINMENT

Audience: Would you aim to mentor family members (in or outside the business), the successor leadership team, other employees, friends, industry contacts, community leaders, aspiring entrepreneurs, disadvantaged youth, or some combination?

Setting: Where would/could you mentor? In person or remotely (much mentorship takes place at a distance these days, thanks to technologies such as Skype)? In an office or some other public venue?

Duration: How long a mentorship relationship are you seeking, bearing in mind that such bonds can last years or even decades?

Goals: How important are concrete goals for you in this context? What goals might you set for the mentorship relationship?

Advice: Where can you get the right advice or guidance for your approach to mentorship, especially if you don't have much experience in this arena? For example, what do you need to learn about maintaining appropriate boundaries, such as ensuring you act as an adviser rather than a decider, or how best to react when your advice isn't taken?

Outcome: Do you need tangible evidence of your influence? How can you feel appreciated even if your advice doesn't match the direction the mentee takes?

Finally, don't forget you can benefit not only as a mentor but as a *mentee*. Jack Herschend, former CEO of Herschend Entertainment, talks about the value in seeking mentors who've already navigated the post-work world as a critical support to this transition process.

> Find a mentor who has already done it. It is not like you sit down one day and draft a plan and then go out and implement it. It's about going through the emotional change and trials and fear and all kinds of stuff that goes through this process, and if you have the right person who has been there and done it you will benefit greatly. I have three times had the chance to be a mentor to men who are going through this. In each case the fear is there - will my wife and I be financially alright? You have to address how you will go from success to significance and make a plan to do that.
>
> **JACK HERSCHEND,** FORMER CEO, HERSCHEND ENTERTAINMENT

Notes

1. John Sutter, "5 Memorable Quotes from Steve Jobs," *CNN.com*, October 6, 2011, http://www.cnn.com/2011/10/05/tech/innovation/steve-jobs-quotes/ (accessed March 15, 2017).
2. Idea of portfolio from David Corbett, *Portfolio Life,* Jossey-Bass, San Francisco, 2012, p. 2.
3. Eli Watkins and Jami Gangel, "George W. Bush Discovers His 'Inner Rembrandt' in Homage to Veterans," *CNN.com*, February 27, 2017, http://www.cnn.com/2017/02/27/politics/george-w-bush-paintings/ (accessed March 15, 2017).

4. George Vaillant, *Aging Well*, Little, Brown, and Company, Boston, 2002, p. 224.
5. Peter Buffett, *Life Is What You Make It*, Crown, 2010, p. 110.
6. Exercise adapted from Hogan, R., & Hogan, J. (2007). Hogan Personality Inventory manual (3rd ed.). Tulsa, OK: Hogan Assessment Systems.
7. For much more on the evidence for and psychology and implications of flow, see Mihaly Csikszentmihalyi, *Flow: The Psychology of Optimal Experience*, Harper Perennial, New York, 2008.

9

Get Around Roadblocks, Assess Your Readiness, and Keep Score

Now that we've covered the key systems and context that play a role in your path ahead, let's consider two important areas related to your sense of progress and fulfillment:

- *The roadblocks you may face*, which often take the form of concerns about your post-work life; and
- *How to measure your impact*, or "keep score" of how far you've come, something that most former business leaders tend to like to do.

This chapter covers both areas in detail.

Identify and Get Around Your Roadblocks

Not surprisingly, there are many spoken and unspoken fears about transitioning away from leadership. How will I fill my days? Will my marriage survive? Will the business or family implode? These fears form roadblocks that may impede your progress, because our tendency is to avoid such concerns by denying they exist or failing to confront them with healthier thoughts and proactive plans. Merely identifying your deeply rooted concerns and the roadblocks they represent is a critical step that can lead to more strategic planning. So, let's consider the main roadblocks transitioning leaders face, and how to deal with them.

Will I Lose All Relevance?

Questions related to his overarching roadblock include:

- Will I still have a voice in the business and family? How much? How will this work?
- Will I be viewed as "out of touch" and uninteresting? Will people still seek my counsel?
- How will I feel if/when the company thrives without me?

As the questions above indicate, this roadblock is about a fear of being "put out to pasture," not surprising given our culture's preference for youth. The reality is that you will have less relevance on some dimensions when you're no longer running a business. So, a large part of overcoming this roadblock is a combination of acceptance (life changes with age) and reframing (each life stage can be dynamic and fulfilling in its own way). You are used to being in the midst of the action, to making important decisions and motivating large groups of people. Losing that sense of relevance can be very threatening, as you think about how to remain relevant without overstepping boundaries.

One helpful point of view on transitions in general is provided by William Bridges, who writes about transitions as being made up of three parts: the ending, the neutral zone, and the new beginning.[1] He makes the important point that people focus excessively on the ending (what's lost) and the new beginning (what's next), rather than understanding there will be an "in-between" that requires adjustment and new thinking: what he calls the neutral zone. That period includes mourning the loss of the past role/activity. Saying goodbye to the past without denying how much it meant to you helps you move more confidently into the future.

Gaining that sense of acceptance enables you to take more practical steps, such as clarifying your core capabilities and interests (see Chapter 8) to understand how you can continue to remain relevant and contribute. Part of this might be working with your successors to determine how and where your voice is needed, for example, on projects or client relationships where your history or knowledge is valuable.

When you are at the start of your leadership tenure try to jot down everything you're changing. Because here is what will happen: Once you retire your successor will come in and change a lot of things as well, and that might tick you off. Not right or wrong, people do things differently. Keep that list of the changes you made at the outset for when you retire and that will help you keep perspective.

PHIL CLEMENS, FORMER CEO OF CLEMENS FAMILY CORPORATION

Getting comfortable with the new reality is important not just for yourself but for others in the systems you inhabit—communicating your comfort and plans for next steps to family, ex-colleagues, friends, and new acquaintances assures people about your status and may help them continue to rely on your insights in meaningful ways, as part of a virtuous cycle. I have found that transitioning leaders who are crystal clear about what they no longer do at the business, and telegraph this to all, enable everyone to find the right way to keep them involved in a new capacity. In a sense, the more clearly you "let go" the easier it will be for the system to leverage your wisdom and insights in a new role—and the more relevance you might have.

Beyond clarifying a role for yourself at the business, your development of new passions and interests may help you bring relevance you hadn't brought before, whether with regard to board service, other forms of leadership/advisory, or pursuit of the arts or other creative activities. In short, the best way to get past the relevance roadblock is to continue to develop yourself and learn. You'll then view the transition not as being put out to pasture but a time of finding *new fields* in which to have impact and grow.

Will the Business and My Family Be Okay?

Related questions here include:

- What will happen to the business when I'm not in charge?
- Can I stay engaged and "out of the way" at the same time? What's the right balance?
- How will relationships with my partner, children, and extended family change?

As with the previous section, these are natural, legitimate concerns that can form a roadblock to action. The reality is that family business CEOs are often the glue or lynchpin for both the family and business. So they and other stakeholders often harbor a real fear that once they retire, the broader systems around them will collapse, stripped of someone with sufficient trust/credibility to keep stakeholders aligned. Indeed, that's often the outcome of poorly planned transitions. Even when a good plan is in place, leaders (and frankly most humans) like to feel that they are indispensable, and that systems won't work well without them—this mentality can create anxiety system-wide.

To address this issue, families can develop strong continuity/transition plans for the business, often with the help of outside consultants.[2] An effective plan includes transparency that helps build confidence about the future among stakeholders. But having a plan on paper doesn't necessarily address underlying fears about how the business and family will function post-change. Nothing can dispel that fully until you get a little lived history under your belt; still, regular communication and meetings between stakeholders are critical to a healthy transition. The exiting leader plays a pivotal role by demonstrating confidence in the future, and serving as "goodwill ambassador" between the company's new leaders and the ownership and broader family systems. Playing this role will help you feel greater optimism about the future, which increases your positive impact further. It's paramount to trust the systems, processes, and people you have developed over the years. Remember that your wisdom is "baked in," and while they may not do everything as you would have, your guidance and teaching undoubtedly help drive key decisions. Communicate your confidence in the system, and set up key parts of it well before you depart—for instance, even if you feel you do not need a board with independent directors, your successors likely will.

On the family side, we discussed the need for intentional transition-related planning in Chapter 5. But it's worth repeating key points here, such as the need to recognize that your marriage will move into a new phase with different routines; working with your spouse to plan proactively will do a great deal to address concerns or bumps along the way. Engage in regular conversations with your partner and broader family about your shared vision for the future. Think about activities you may want to pursue together but also time you may need for yourself. How will daily routines change or clash? It may even be worth proactively seeking counseling with your partner or family, to work through the expected changes and develop shared expectations and a plan.

In short, take this planning seriously. Set aside regular times for it. Ask questions and listen. Anticipate, rather than denying anxiety, then work through it together. Be intentional.

Will I Be Bored?

Related questions include:

- Will I find new opportunities I like?
- Will my days be completely unstructured?
- How will I keep learning/growing?

Under-stimulation is a large, reasonable concern for those who've been busy for decades. Fear of boredom, after all, is a close cousin of fear of irrelevance. Driven leaders lack skill at standing still, which is why I've mentioned repeatedly in this book that I'm concerned for leaders whose post-work plan is some unstructured notion of "travel and leisure." In all likelihood, that's not enough.

Hopefully this book has provided ideas and examples of paths CEOs have taken to find genuine purpose and fulfillment, along with improving their golf game for some. But it won't just happen. Just as you had to engage in planning to execute strategy in business, planning your personal future requires "big picture" visioning, selection of options, and implementation. At the same time, I've seen too many new ex-CEOs jump on *every* possible opportunity, perhaps driven by fear of irrelevance, then feel overwhelmed. The trick is finding the balance between too little and too much, as we'll discuss more in a bit.

Part of the problem is that while we humans are staying healthier and vital longer than ever, many of us still have a script or stereotypical image of a "retiree"—someone with little to do but bide their time as year after uneventful year passes. You need to identify any such misconceptions you may hold, and work to get past them, while taking real steps to structure your rich, engaged post-work life.

So take the time to clarify your goals and the *balance* you want at this new stage. How much time do you want to allocate to work, to family, to new initiatives, to service, to learning, to play, to whatever else? Be honest with yourself about what you need and want in terms of the pace of your days, and what that means for involvement with individuals and organizations.

Will I Lose Autonomy?

Some sub-questions related to this theme are:

- Will I feel (or be viewed) as "old" and "useless?"
- Will my health fail me?
- Will lost autonomy hasten my demise?

Part of the reason this transition out of career is so emotionally challenging is that it's inexorably tied to later life stages, which naturally brings up fears related to anticipated physical or mental decline—and, ultimately, mortality. Many driven professionals fear that if they slow their pace at all from 100 miles per hour they'll drop straight to 0, their mind and body giving out, leaving only a shadow of their former self. Feeding into this are the stories of hard-charging CEOs who did indeed retire and die too quickly, suggesting the validity of death by deceleration. It may not be the norm, but it does happen.

As with everything here, your attitude will make a difference. If you consider this transition proactively and look forward to all the opportunities and adventures you can now pursue, it can be liberating and energizing. In fact, I have seen that individuals who plan for their retirement find far more satisfaction in that life-stage than those who leave work involuntarily, whether due to poor health or some mandatory retirement age.

Beyond attitude, your physical health will play a large role. Not surprisingly, taking proactive steps by keeping fit and staying engaged can only help. Then, when you do arrive at a point where your health or energy compromises your options, having taken time along the way to develop a broader range of interests and passions will pay off in the form of greater opportunities, including those that don't require peak physical condition. This might mean transitioning from a daily tennis match to regular walks with friends, or moving from serving on three corporate boards to informally advising several younger executives in your network.

Acceptance is critical here. As the Serenity Prayer suggests, change what you can, accept what you can't, and learn to recognize the difference.

Will I Find Balance?

Sub-questions here include:

- Will I be too busy or not busy enough?
- Will I struggle to balance what I "should" do with what I want to do?

- Will I find the right proportion of activities involving family, other collaborative pursuits, and independent activities?

One of the benefits of leading a family business is that this complex role has likely taught you much about balancing competing interests and priorities, along with how to manage paradoxes. Draw on this skill-set to ease the transition to a fulfilling post-leadership life.

To carry the analogy further, it can be helpful to think of life's varied activities as representing a *portfolio*: family, board opportunities, mentorship, volunteering, personal enrichment, travel. Be intentional about what activities you want in your portfolio, keeping in mind the idea of balance. For example, one challenge is balancing your individual needs and those of your broader family. You may feel ready for retirement but your son/successor may not be ready to take the reins just yet, and may pressure you to delay. Similarly, you may want to start a new business and serve on five boards, but your spouse may want you to take time off and join her in training for senior triathlons.

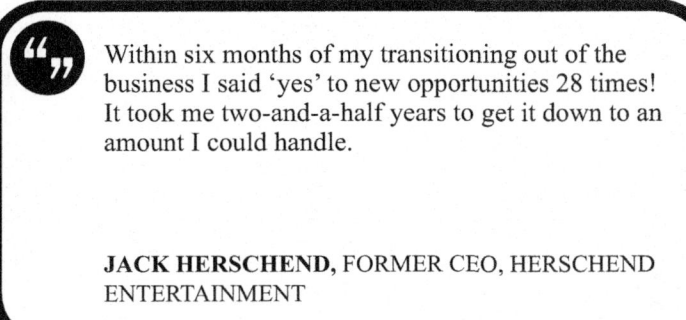

Within six months of my transitioning out of the business I said 'yes' to new opportunities 28 times! It took me two-and-a-half years to get it down to an amount I could handle.

JACK HERSCHEND, FORMER CEO, HERSCHEND ENTERTAINMENT

This relates to the idea of balancing what you *want* to do with what you feel you *should* do. Here again, there's no simple answer but fortunately, you have a lifetime of experience assessing such trade-offs on multiple dimensions and making decisions. Still, the only way to manage this complex balancing act is to get very clear on *what you want*, to more easily understand where to compromise and where to stand your ground. That plays into another paradox here: the tension between your sense of duty and your actual desires. For example, what are some responsibilities you feel you "should" take on—whether to facilitate the transition or perhaps because you are best-suited to the role—and how much do these "demands" reduce your opportunity to pursue other priorities? For example, if you feel you need to serve as board chair of your family firm to reassure the ownership group that they'll still have your counsel, you may be limiting your option to serve on other boards, establish a foundation, or relocate to a warmer climate. The "Talk About Competing Needs" box has tips for communicating on trade-offs with those affected.

Table 9.1: Talk About Competing Needs

Follow these guidelines to have frank, inclusive conversations about balancing your needs with others' in your family, business or broader community:

1. *Get clear on what you want:* You can't engage in productive thinking about shared interests until you have clarity on your own. Take the time to consider what your needs and priorities are today and what they'll likely be in the future.

2. *Ask questions instead of making assumptions:* Humans fall into the assumptions trap all the time, especially with close others. You may have been married for 40 years, but you still may not know your partners' hopes and dreams unless you ask. Asking them shows you care, and gets them thinking about what they want, independent of what you want, to make better joint decisions.

3. *Listen:* Leaders are used to getting input and making decisions. Here, you may not be the ultimate or only 'decider,' but getting and listening to input will help you balance your goals with those of others close to you.

4. *Collaborate:* Think about how to align interests and build plans/options that are feasible and fulfilling to everyone involved.

Plan Strategically, Expect the Unexpected

Finally, one of the most important paradox-related skills you may need to call on is the ability to plan for the future while appreciating that things don't always go according to plan. You may plan to spend more time traveling and then find that a string of acquisitions calls on you to be in town for board meetings more often than expected. Or you may hope to engage your favorite non-profit in an exciting new initiative, only to find that you cannot get full buy-in from that board. Or you may be poised to go into business with an old buddy on a vineyard, until he becomes seriously, unexpectedly ill. Life has a nasty habit of throwing us curveballs, and perhaps somewhat more so as we get older in life. None of that should preclude you from planning but should merely serve as a reminder that—just like in business—the best laid plans rarely unfold exactly as scripted.

Despite knowing this, people routinely neglect to plan for retirement, in part because of all it represents (as covered throughout this book), in part because of the very real demands of family business leadership—urgent trumps important nearly 100% of the time. Taking the time to plan helps anticipate and address the complex changes that will occur in the overlapping systems, while aligning key stakeholders in the family and business around what to expect and how to do their part. The "Plan for Your Plan" box offers practical tips for planning out this critical phase of life.

Table 9.2: Plan for Your Plan

Approach your post-work plan much like you would the strategic planning for your business. Ideally you can pull together some trusted advisors and friends you can rely on for input into your plan, especially those who have already retired and/or can call you out on questionable elements of your plan. Include the following elements:

Vision: What's the overall vision for what you want post-work life to look like? How realistic is this? Can you craft a 'vision statement' for your personal future?

Buckets: What are the 'buckets' through which this vision will come to life: professional, community, philanthropy, family, others?

Time: How will you will allocate time to these buckets, much as you would allocate capital for a business? Consider your key drivers and what you will find more motivating, as well as what is realistic. You should expect your time allocations to vary along this journey, so put in place a mechanism to review this annually (again, like a budget).

Tactics: What tactics will best support the vision? How can you use them strategically?

Collaborators: How can you involve your spouse, family, friends, and others in the planning process and the actual plan?

KPIs: What key performance indicators will help you track progress and "keep score," whether measures of your impact, balance, relationship harmony, or others? (more on this later in the chapter)

Review/revision: How often will you review and revise your plan, to optimize it?

Assess Your Readiness and Set Goals

How ready are you and the systems you inhabit to move forward?

Throughout this book, we have spoken about a number of aspects of "readiness" critical to successful transition from your family business leadership role. If you have not really begun the planning process in earnest, a good first step can be to use the ideas here to engage in an informal assessment around your readiness for this change.

As part of this process, consider where you may need to do the most work to make this process go smoothly. For example, how much is your identity anchored in your professional role? How hard is it for you to make changes in general? How will your physical health or attitude help/hinder this process? Certainly, there are some aspects of your personal, family, or business readiness that are easier to change than others. For example, you can proactively seek to develop new interests more easily than you can "will yourself" to be healthier. No matter the dimension, take the time to make a clear assessment of the strengths and limitations you face, to anticipate and look for solutions to challenges while also developing some self-empathy.

As a good way to pull together the ideas and learning from this book, use Table 9.3 to engage in a simple "readiness assessment" diagnosis based on the key indicators that we have reviewed. These dimensions reflect the conceptual model—so more details on each idea would be found in Chaps. 3 and 4 for personal, Chapter 5 on family, and Chapter 6 on the business. It may be helpful if you complete this form and then ask a variety of stakeholders for feedback on some or all dimensions, to get additional perspectives and insight on your 'readiness'.

In completing the assessment, be as honest with yourself as possible about all parts, hopefully using some of the ideas in this book and brainstorming with other people. Then use the information you've gathered to help shape your plan. How much work is needed to strengthen your family and business systems? With whom should you collaborate? Set a series of concrete goals and timetables to put the structures in place that will support success at all levels. Strike the right balance between working on some low-hanging fruit (items where change is needed but is not anticipated to be too difficult) to build momentum, with a dose of clear planning for the bigger obstacles. Work with advisors or consult good resources to support the work you may need to do to get the family and business systems ready. Many books and articles have been referenced throughout this book and a full list of these resources can be found in the "Recommended Reading and Other Resources" section at the back of this book.

Table 9.3: Overall Readiness Assessment

Using a scale of 1 to 5, Please use the first column to 'score' the level of readiness you perceive in each of the core dimensions of the model that has been discussed in this book. Use the same scale to indicate how hard you think it will be to make any needed changes in that dimension and use the third column to note some ideas for progress.

DIMENSION	READINESS SCORE Scale of 1 to 5 1 = There is a lot of change needed here, to 5 = Excellent, feels 'ready'	EASE TO ADDRESS Scale of 1 to 5 1 = Will be very hard to change, to 5 = Can and already is changing	IDEAS FOR HOW TO MOVE FORWARD
INTERNAL			
Identity: Job no longer as central to your sense of 'self'			
Temperament: Open to new experiences & need for control			
Change Capacity: Ease in letting go of goals & developing new ones			
FAMILY			
Relationships: Strong marriage and family bonds			
Healthy/effective communication			
BUSINESS			
Ownership alignment			
Financial/market strength of enterprise			
Successor team strength			
Strength/depth of governance systems			

I advocate setting "SMART" goals: those that are specific, measurable, achievable, realistic, and time bound. For example, "getting in better shape" is a goal but not a particularly SMART one, as it lacks several of the dimensions in the acronym. "Being able to run three miles in 30 minutes three months from now" is a much SMARTer goal.

Remember: while the systems around you may facilitate (or hinder) the process, your personal readiness falls squarely on your shoulders. If you anticipate struggling on many of the "internal readiness" dimensions, it may be important to work with a coach, mentor, close friend, or professional counselor on the transition—though it might be difficult to summon the will to do this, especially at first. Just as with changes to the business or family systems, you can set clear goals for yourself on evolution along these dimensions, to track your progress and address the needed changes in smaller, more digestible increments. Chapter 10 has additional ideas for how to get started down this path.

Keeping Score

Finally, it's important to articulate your personal measures of success in this new life stage—the "M" in SMART goals as described above. The saying "What gets measured gets improved" is very apt here. On the one hand, in retirement you have the luxury of no longer being bound by the kinds of metrics you faced as a business leader: revenues, growth, profits, ROI, and the like. But on the other, you may lose windows into the value of your efforts on multiple fronts because you no longer need to translate them into quantifiable results.

Keeping "score" of your progress in some form can be helpful. You've worked under some kind of scoring system most of your life, so continuing that can help you make and see progress, reflect on your contributions, and feel valued. In addition, in my experience, business leaders tend to be competitive by nature—they like a challenge, and want to know how they are measuring up to that challenge. If you know this kind of thinking drives you, it may be even more important that you develop a way to "keep score."

How exactly you do that is up to you. For example, my partner Jim's grandfather actively competed in senior Olympics throughout his retirement—relishing the thrill of competition to measure his performance in athletic pursuits. Think about the categories that matter most to you from the list that follows and others, then develop an informal system for measuring your impact and progress in each:

- learning (as related to enrichment activities, for example)
- personal growth
- fitness
- progress of any organizations you're part of (on multiple dimensions)
- engagement with family
- community impact (including philanthropy).

How exactly you measure progress on these or other dimensions is up to you, whether through a quantitative indicator or less formal means ("poor-good-excellent"). You can also decide how often to keep score, but I recommend at least every six months. At that time, you can also reassess which goals continue to matter to you, and which you may want to discard, intensify, or add.

Irv Robinson, former CEO of Robbie Fantastic Flexibles, offers good perspective on the "keeping score" part of personal continuity.

> If your work is in the non-profit world, most of those organizations have enough structure that you can measure success, such as if the budget goes from X to Y and you were part of that. But where it gets a little more difficult to measure is whether you've made relationships that matter to you better. It's kind of like building a culture in a business. There isn't a financial statement item on culture - but there are indicators and you can create indicators that need to be hit, like whether you made a difference in someone's life. You have to be a little bit creative about that to develop some benchmarks for yourself.
>
> **IRV ROBINSON,** CO-FOUNDER AND FORMER CEO OF ROBBIE FANTASTIC FLEXIBLES

Beyond keeping score on your own, consider working with mentors, advisors, friends, or other confidants to hold yourself accountable, share success, and solve problems that may come up. It's a great way to collaborate, learn, and grow.

Notes

1. For much more on understanding and dealing with life transitions, see William Bridges, *Transitions: Making Sense of Life's Changes*, DeCapo, Cambridge, 2004.
2. For much more on effective succession planning, see Kelly Lecouvie and Jennifer Pendergast, *Family Business Succession: Your Roadmap to Continuity*, Palgrave Macmillan, New York, 2014.

10

Conclusion

As this book comes to a close, I hope you have captured some good ideas and inspiration to move forward with active planning for your life's next important chapter. Although all the topics we discussed could be explored in greater depth, my hope was to provide an overview to stimulate your thinking about your personal passions, goals, and plans, and to encourage some good conversations with your family, colleagues, and advisors to support this important dimension of continuity planning as it relates to the entire family enterprise.

What struck me in the interviews with successful CEOs who have navigated this transition was the extent to which most had nurtured outside interests alongside their work obligations throughout the course of their career. I hope this encourages younger readers to ensure they have interests beyond just work, and motivates advisors and mentors to support this in their younger charges. Not only does this help aid the transition out of leadership; in my view, it adds to the insights and perspectives leaders bring to their day job as well.

> If you are only retiring from your organization you will always look at that with regret. What are you retiring to?
>
> **PHIL CLEMENS,** FORMER CEO CLEMENS FAMILY CORPORATION

For those of you reading this who have not had the interest or ability to pursue much beyond building your business for many years, I hope this book has provided some ideas on how to reframe your passions and skills into domains outside of work where you could continue to make a difference and find reward. Whether you have a natural portfolio of passions already in mind or need to think through how to best deploy your time and talents, as was touched on in Chaps. 8 and 9, to move into the deliberate stage of this process, you need to engage in some personal strategic planning.

I always cultivated activities and passions that involved my family, like boating or skiing or traveling. We did these a bit together along the way, and this tradition has grown into more opportunities for connection now that I have more flexibility.

DICK DEVOS, FORMER PRESIDENT OF AMWAY

Get Clear on What You Want

While I sincerely hope that the ideas and tools in this book will help you down this path, there is nothing that can really replace "quiet thinking." This can be a challenge for hard-driving CEOs who are very oriented to action—but spending a little time with your thoughts and in reflection is a powerful investment in getting to real clarity about what YOU want. While I have stressed throughout this book that this process doesn't happen in a vacuum, you can't factor in the other parts of the system until you have clarity on your own needs. Think about your journey, be honest with yourself, and take yourself to a place where you have traditionally done your best deep thinking. To paraphrase the journalist David Brooks—give some thought to your "eulogy values,"[1] or what matters most deeply to you.

It is worth pointing out that in addition to the remarkable diversity of passions and non-work commitments I heard about from the interviewees, I was also struck by the extent to which most of these successful business leaders were anchored by a guiding philosophy of life that is broader than just bottom-line thinking. Most of these individuals are either deeply anchored by their faith or a clear sense of their "why" or purpose beyond the scope of their professional success. Reflecting on your sense of purpose, and expanding your view or definition of this if it has been largely work anchored, might well be critically important to this process.

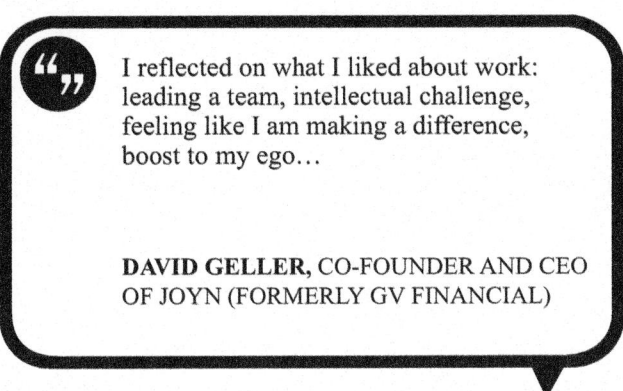

> I reflected on what I liked about work: leading a team, intellectual challenge, feeling like I am making a difference, boost to my ego…
>
> **DAVID GELLER,** CO-FOUNDER AND CEO OF JOYN (FORMERLY GV FINANCIAL)

Having said that, one of my primary goals for this book is to foster empathy and understanding about this process. As was underscored in Chapter 1, change is hard and this particular change is really hard! The mini assessments and tips throughout this book are not meant to either give you a free pass ("this is uniquely hard for me, so I can skip it…"), or beat yourself up on some sort of "limitation" you believe you have—they are to help you and others better appreciate why and how this journey and planning is hard for so many. If you feel stuck in your thinking about what you want for this stage of your life, make a point of seeking help and support in delving through these questions.

Get Aligned with Others on the Path Forward

Once you have had the quiet time to gain clarity on your true hopes and goals, it is time to weave that into the broader tapestry of your family and business. Talk about your vision with all affected stakeholders, give them a chance to share their concerns and hopes for the future—and listen to what they have to say. Ensure that you have the systems in place that will support the needs of the business and the family as these organizations envision and plan for a future with new leaders at the helm.

> What I did more than anything else is to ask 'what things would have to be in place to make you comfortable about transitioning' - I am deeply grateful that I have been given the longevity that I have had - that was the important part of my journey - having a clear vision of what I wanted the company to look like. I think I am leaving better leadership than I provided.
>
> **JIM ETHIER,** FORMER CHAIRMAN & CEO, BUSH BROTHERS & COMPANY

Getting all affected stakeholders aligned and comfortable with the path forward is no small task—and again, this book merely touches on the many topics that come up as a leader is transitioning. Hopefully, the tips and other resources shared in these chapters are helpful to advancing the thinking and planning that goes into this process for all.

Develop a Plan and Commit to the Plan

Once you have a vision and some clear goals in mind, and have coordinated as needed with your family and business, it can be helpful to engage in deliberate strategic planning. Make a plan that includes clarity on the resources you will need to have success with your goals. Put the needed resources in place, pursue additional resources and connections you may need, and get clear on the indicators you will use to track your progress and success. To the extent that you can (bearing in mind the "best laid plans tend to evolve when confronted with the real world"), put your thoughts, goals, and plans into writing. Ensuring that your personal continuity planning in the context of your transition away from the leadership of the business is well understood by stakeholders is important.

In my experience, business leaders like to keep score, and are comfortable with yardsticks that help them track how they are doing. Depending on what you are pursuing, it may take some effort and creative thinking to delineate the "measurable outcomes" you want at this stage of your journey, but I believe it is worth clarifying this to increase your sense of accomplishment and satisfaction. In addition, the use of clear goals and targets will help you hold yourself accountable to the process, and allow you to evaluate your progress.

Give yourself permission to go as big or as small as fits your vision, energy, and passions. One of the CEOs I interviewed, Jack Cakebread, is likely better known for the business he established as part of his "next" stage of life… so, you never know where your "wild idea" might take you or others.

Dad started Cakebread garage in the mid 1920s in Oakland and worked there for 50 years. I also made my career there but had a passion for photography and was fortunate enough to have worked with Ansel Adams for 11 years.

It was when I was on a photo assignment photographing winemakers that I fell in love that that process. A friend of our family had a cow pasture up the road from the Mondavi vineyard and that is how I got into wine…. For years of course we did both – run the garage, while starting the wine endeavor – but I had a vision that this is where I wanted to put my energies, so I sold the auto shop to my employees eventually to be able to pursue this full-time.

JACK CAKEBREAD, FOUNDER AND HONORARY CHAIRMAN OF CAKEBREAD CELLARS, DESCRIBING HOW HE GOT INTO THE WINE INDUSTRY AS A SECOND CAREER/PASSION.

Evaluate and Adapt as Needed

As you know from leading business, all planning does require evaluation and evolution as realities shift around you. When you are clear on what you are pursuing and the indicators you use for success, you can adapt the actions and commitments you make as needed when circumstances change, as they will over time.

Ensure you also have the support you need. Developing and strengthening your social and professional network will ensure you have access to opportunities and adequate fun and human connection at this next stage of life. In addition, you may want to build a "personal board of advisors" who can be sounding boards for your efforts and priorities going forward. Some of the CEOs with whom I spoke had this in a group of respected peers, others developed it through their family council (council of elders), and yet others simply relied on their spouse for this critical support.

So many of us are fortunate to be living in a time and place that allows us to explore new challenges and opportunities well into our twilight years. With our expanded life expectancy and better health, my hope is that we can leverage the experience and knowledge we have gained on life's journey to date and use that to explore new roads and horizons to find fulfillment and make a positive impact on others.

Best of luck on this exciting next chapter of your journey—may you find great opportunities and traveling companions that add to your joy!

Note

1. David Brooks TED talk (March 2014) Should you live for your resume… or your eulogy? https://www.ted.com/talks/david_brooks_should_you_live_for_your_resume_or_your_eulogy

Appendix 1: Brief Interviewee Profiles

Eric Allyn, Welch Allyn

About the Company

- Founded in 1915 by Dr. Francis Welch and William Noah Allyn.
- Welch Allyn is a premier developer and manufacturer of medical devices, producing instruments such as ophthalmoscopes, otoscopes, blood pressure gauges, thermometers, ECGs, and multi-parameter monitors.
- The company's products are ubiquitous, found in virtually every hospital and physician office in the USA, and in nearly every country worldwide.
- In 2015, after four generations of Allyn family ownership, Welch Allyn was sold to Hill-Rom, which retained the Welch Allyn name and expanded its operations and market presence globally.

About the Interviewee

Eric Allyn, great-grandson of co-founder William Noah Allyn, worked as a part-time/summer employee with Welch Allyn from 1982 to 1989, then as a full-time employee and executive from 1990 to 2009.

In 2009, the family shareholders asked Eric if he would be willing to step away from his responsibilities in management to serve on the board of directors, as their family policy would preclude him from serving in both capacities, and his experience was needed at the board. From 2009 to 2015 he served on the board of directors, including as co-chairman from 2010 to 2015, when the family sold the business.

Eric's Tips for Successful Transition

- Be sure that you leave behind a functional organization, particularly from a governance perspective. Without this, it's hard for the business to continue to grow, and the lack of it is likely to create conflict.
- Aim for a multi-year transition for yourself. Consider taking some board positions outside of the family business before leaving the family business.
- In general, seek to build a new network and reputation outside the family business before leaving.

Murray Berstein, Nixon Uniform Service and Medical Wear

About the Company[1]

- Founded in 1967 by Murray Berstein and his brother as a dry-cleaning business, Nixon evolved into a textile rental company, with a focus on clothing for the healthcare market.
- Today, Nixon provides and manages a professional apparel and medical linen service for outpatient healthcare practices.
- The business employs over 400 people and serves over 8500 customers weekly in the US Northeast, Mid-Atlantic, and Southwest.

About the Interviewee

Murray started Nixon with his brother, growing the business into a significant regional player. After he and his brother parted ways, Murray set up a board of directors, where he served as executive chair for many years. In the early 2000s, Murray hired an advisor to help him think about how to best transition the business to his sons. They worked as a family to get the business and stakeholders ready for this transition, and Murray gave up his leadership role about ten years ago, stepping into the role of chairman emeritus two years ago, in 2015.

Among other activities he has pursued in retirement, Murray has a special interest in helping a local high school increase graduation rates.

Murray's Tips for Successful Transition

- "Begin with the end in mind," especially if you're fortunate to have strong options for a successor. Put a board of directors or advisors in place that the next generation would respect and eventually help to reselect.
- About 15 years before you would think it necessary, encourage the next generation to help choose a succession/transition consultant specialized in privately owned businesses.
- Be financially secure before you let go. Don't depend on your former business for your financial well-being.
- Find a new passion. It's lonely when you leave one of the major reasons that made you feel accomplished. I chose boating, volunteering at schools, and tackling home repairs.

Jack Cakebread, Cakebread Cellars

About the Company

- Cakebread Cellears was founded in 1973 by Jack and Dolores Cakebread—when they purchased 22 acres near a friend's property to pursue a passion for winemaking.
- Located near Rutherford in the heart of the Napa Valley, Cakebread Cellars remains family owned and operated.
- Today, Cakebread Cellars owns over 1100 acres with 560 of those planted to vineyards with a focus on making fine, handmade wines. The company employs about 75 people, growing to 125 employees during seasonal peaks.

About the Interviewee

Jack Cakebread's father was an entrepreneur, starting Cakebread Garage in the mid-1920s—where Jack also made his first career. However, Jack had other important interests and projects—including photography. It was while on a photo assignment that he fell in love with winemaking, and the idea of pursuing this craft took shape. To make this vision a reality, Jack and Delores purchased 22 acres in the Napa Valley, and would head out there every weekend to nurture this vision, all while Jack was still running the garage for several years.

Today, Jack and Delores remain the moral core of the business they started. Jack transitioned to honorary chair of the board in 2012, but he had released operational control to their sons many years earlier. Their sons, Dennis (chairman of the board and responsible for sales and marketing) and Bruce, president and CEO, have operated the winery for a number of years. Jack takes pride in watching the continued progress and growth of the winery.

Jack's Tips for Successful Transition

- It's not so hard; just get started on your transition instead of putting it off, the earlier the better.
- Leverage your wisdom and continue to engage, the most recent insights you develop are informed by everything you have done before and can often be the most powerful.

Marilyn Carlson Nelson, Carlson

About the Company[2]

- The Carlson company grew out of the Minneapolis-based Gold Bond Stamp Company founded by Curtis Carlson in 1938.
- Now in its third generation of closely held family ownership, Carlson operates in more than 150 countries and territories throughout the world.
- A global leader in the travel industry, the foundation of the Carlson portfolio of businesses is the world's premier business and travel management company, Carlson Wagonlit Travel.
- More than 170,000 employees in 160 countries work under the Carlson brands, which include Radisson and Regent hotels, Country Inns & Suites, Park Inn, Park Plaza, Carlson Wagonlit Travel, Carlson Marketing and T.G.I. Fridays restaurants.

About the Interviewee

Marilyn Carlson Nelson is the daughter of founder Curtis Carlson and former chair and CEO of the company. Marilyn took on that role at age 59 and made a personal commitment to herself that she would stay in the position no longer than ten years—to bridge the first generation to the third generation of stewardship. Under her leadership, company revenues doubled to $40 billion.

Today, Marilyn remains a co-owner of Carlson Holdings, Inc., and is an advisor to the company, describing herself as "listener-in-chief" and full-time head cheerleader. Her daughter Diana Nelson is current chair of the board.

Outside the company, Marilyn finds deep reward engaging her leadership experience and the relationships built over a lifetime in issues about which she cares deeply—human rights, the arts, and the economic vitality of communities and the spread of democracy worldwide. In addition, she appreciates having the time to reflect, to appreciate the deep insights that "perspective" gives to us all, and to share that with others.

Marilyn's Tip for Successful Transition

It has been said, "There are two lasting bequests we can give our children. One is roots, the other wings." If your family values have been embedded in the culture of the company, let go, so that those values can be made relevant for the times.

Phil Clemens, the Clemens Family Corporation

About the Company[3]

- Founded in 1895 by John C. Clemens, Phil's grandfather, with a firm grounding in the values of ethics, integrity, and stewardship.
- Today the Clemens Family Corporation is a food company with a full-line pork production and processing operation and a real estate development and holding company. The company is best known for its legacy brand: Hatfield.
- The company remains based in Pennsylvania but has a national reach, with about 2500 employees. Projected revenues for 2017 were in excess of $800 million.

About the Interviewee

Phil literally grew up in the business (his family home was on the property when he was born), and made his full career at the family company. After working within the human resources areas of the firm for 20 years, Phil served as CEO of the Clemens Family Corporation from 1995 to 2017. Today, Phil is a member of his family's family council—the group that works on family matters, not business issues, investing in harmony and connectedness.

In addition to the many civic and business projects that Phil pursues through board service and others, he describes himself as a "family ambassador," helping family businesses around the globe by sharing his family's story of how they transitioned from being a family business to being a business family.

Phil's Tips for Successful Transition

- Be very intentional.
- As the leader, be a resource to an independent committee that will choose your successor. But don't pick your successor.
- Be willing to help your successor—*if asked*. Be a cheerleader for your successor and get out of their way.

Lanse Crane, Crane & Company

About the Company

- Founded in 1770 by Stephen Crane in Dalton, Massachusetts.
- Crane creates 100% cotton paper that is engrained into American history, including as the paper used by Paul Revere for his engraved banknotes to fund the revolution.
- Crane today is a global currency company supplying security features, banknote paper, and printed currency to governments worldwide.
- The business is a currency industry leader in innovation and security technology. Profitable and growing, Crane also continues to supply the US government with all its paper requirements for printing US currency, as it has continuously since 1879.

About the Interviewee

Lanse Crane had a successful career as an attorney before he was tapped to become the CEO of Crane & Company in 1995. He served as chairman and CEO from 1995 to 2006, stepping down from the role of chairman while the board conducted a search for his successor. Today, Lanse is an engaged shareholder of Crane but otherwise has no formal role.

As a past chair and CEO, he strives to be visibly supportive of strategies where possible, and shares any constructive concerns privately with leadership to provide them the benefit of his experience and judgment, without undermining their leadership.

Beyond Crane, Lanse has built a career as a board chair and director of private companies, particularly multi-generational family businesses of scale. In this capacity, he strives to offer ownership and management the benefit of his experience with the challenges of owning and operating legacy family businesses—especially those of going through significant transitions of ownership, strategy, and/or leadership.

Lanse's Tips for Successful Transition

- For the business, remember there are no "fingerprints" on success, and effective succession can only be achieved when successors are provided ample space to develop and opportunity to grow.
- For the individual, develop new interests and opportunities to contribute post-transition in meaningful and rewarding ways.

Dick DeVos, Amway

About the Company[4]

- Founded in 1959 in Ada, Michigan, by Jay Van Adel and Rich DeVos.
- Amway is a family-owned business that manufactures high-quality consumer products in the beauty, nutrition, and housewares categories.
- All products are sold exclusively through Amway Business Owners. The business was built with the goal of helping others succeed with a business of their own, through the "power of relationships."
- Today, Amway is a multibillion-dollar business with over 10,000 employees operating across over 100 countries and territories.

About the Interviewee

Dick is the son of Amway co-founder Rich DeVos, and served as the company's CEO from 1993 to 2002, after holding roles in multiple areas within the firm. Amway pursued extensive global expansion under Dick's leadership. He left the CEO role at the age of 48, though remains an engaged owner and advisor to the enterprise.

Prior to stepping into the leadership role at Amway, Dick served for two years as the CEO of the family's Orlando Magic NBA basketball franchise. Reflecting the diversity of his interests and priorities, shortly after leaving the Amway role, Dick ran for governor of the state of Michigan in 2006, and he and his family continue to be active in government and policy work. Today, in addition to his civic pursuits and time with family, Dick pursues a variety of business opportunities through his Windquist Group investment management firm.

Dick's Tips for Successful Transition

- Plan carefully.
- Commit to waiting six months without agreeing to another engagement, whether in a business or non-profit role.
- Allow yourself to truly process your passion for the next "chapter" of your life.

Jim Ethier, Bush Brothers & Company

About the Company[5]

- Founded in 1908 by Andrew Jackson Bush as a Tennessee-based tomato cannery.
- Bush Brothers & Company offers a large variety of canned vegetables and other products, and is the US's leading producer of branded bean products.
- The company is headquartered in Knoxville, Tennessee, with production locations in Chestnut Hill, Tennessee, and Augusta, Wisconsin.
- The business employs around 700 people.

About the Interviewee

Jim is a third-generation member of the Bush family and served as chairman & CEO of Bush Brothers from 2003 until 2009, having previously been president and COO of the company. After he helped the business hire its first non-family CEO in 2009, Jim became board chairman from that year to 2012, departing the role at age 69—explicitly with the intent of setting a precedent for retirement before the age of 70.

Today, Jim remains a board director and member of the nominating/governance committee of the board. In addition, he has participated in the food industry as a board member of the Grocery Manufacturers Association and board member and chair of the Food Products Association.

Outside of this industry, Jim serves on several boards and spends time consulting with family businesses and lecturing at college and graduate school programs. He is an adjunct professor at Northwestern University's Kellogg School program for family business.

Jim's Tips for Successful Transition

- Set a target date for retirement early on.
- Develop a full list of objectives that need to be concluded before leaving.

David Geller, JOYN

About the Company[6]

- Founded by brothers David and Matthew Geller in 1991.
- JOYN is an independent registered investment advisor with a unique focus on behavioral wealth management, which links behavioral economics and behavioral finance.
- The business serves the needs of high-net worth individuals and family businesses, with over $1 billion in assets under management.

About the Interviewee

David Geller is the co-founder and CEO of JOYN, known as GV Financial until 2016. He started his career at the Atlanta-based law firm Powell, Goldstein, Frazer & Murphy (now Bryan Cave), before entering the financial planning field in 1986 and co-founding JOYN with his brother in 1991.

While David remains CEO of the business, he was a "fit" for this project because he elected to take a six-month sabbatical from his work, to consider how his work fit into the broader portfolio of his life, modeling what he wants his clients to do: take steps to ensure their work and wealth are developed in service of their broader sense of purpose and joy.

David's Tips for Successful Transition

- Create liquidity outside of the business so you are not financially dependent on the business to fund your retirement.
- Once you are gone, let your successors do what they think is best.
- Offer advice only when asked.

Jack Herschend, Herschend Family Entertainment

About the Company

- Herschend Family Entertainment was founded in Branson, Missouri, by brothers Jack and Pete Herschend.
- Today, the company is headquartered in Atlanta, Georgia; it creates, develops, and operates entertainment, tourism, and hospitality properties, such as Dollywood, Silver Dollar City, and Splash Island.
- Herschend properties span 26 locations across nine US states, attracting over 13 million visitors annually. In addition, HFE owns the Harlem Globetrotters—bringing that special athletic brand of family entertainment to audiences worldwide.

About the Interviewee

Jack Herschend is co-founder and co-owner of Herschend Family Entertainment (HFE), formerly Silver Dollar City, Inc. He is chairman emeritus of the board of directors of HFE and previously served as chairman, president and CEO of the organization.

He was president of Silver Dollar City, Inc., from 1967 until it became Herschend Family Entertainment, of which he was CEO. At the age of 68, he transitioned out of this role (though he returned for a one-year stint five years later at the request of the board), and today attends board meetings as an interested family member. Beyond his interest in HFE, Jack spends a great deal of time mentoring leaders involved in various ministries, with a special focus on those involved with youth and strengthening families.

Jack's Tips for Successful Transition

- Retire to serve other purposes about which you are passionate.
- Savor time with family and close others in your community.

David Juday, IDEAL Industries

About the Company

- A family-owned and controlled company for over 100 years.
- IDEAL is based on a core business of wholesale distribution to professional electrician customers.
- The company has additional business lines in retail products and Original Equipment Manufacturing (OEM) including data communications tools and supplies, tools for professional automotive techs, environmental monitoring equipment, and OEM products for alternative energy management
- The business has 1300 employees operating in manufacturing plants in the USA, Canada, UK, and China.

About the Interviewee

David Juday was named Chairman at IDEAL at the age of 39, after having held positions in manufacturing, IT, sales, and marketing. He served in this leadership role for 30 years, having made a firm commitment to himself to transition out before age 70. Today, David continues to serve as a director at IDEAL, and has taken on several special projects, including the construction of a new plant and working on family estate planning. He is active in the committees that do the work of family governance.

The Juday family has deep ties in Northern Wisconsin, and David serves on the local economic development corporation there. This led to his purchase of a factory building that is now used as a business incubator in the region. In addition, David has invested in other facilities to support the growth of other businesses, and works as an advisor to a number of these business ventures.

David's Tips for Successful Transition

- Be very deliberate in your planning process and more deliberate in executing on it.
- If in your musings about retirement you think you might have made a bigger contribution than some of the previous generations, you need to realize that this is not an accomplishment but rather an absolute *requirement* if the company is to move from generation to generation.
- You need to get out of the way because the next generation is going to have to improve on whatever it is that you did.

Irv Robinson, Robbie Fantastic Flexibles

About the Company

- Founded in 1970 in downtown Kansas City by Bernard Robinson and his son Irv, to leverage the innovation of using perforated plastic wrap on produce.
- Today, Robbie is a manufacturer and printer of flexible packaging for food and non-food retail products, with customers including supermarket chains, food processors, and consumer product companies.
- Robbie was acquired by Canada's largest printing company in mid-2016.
- The company has over 180 employees at its headquarters in Lenexa, Kansas.

About the Interviewee

Irv co-founded Robbie Fantastic Flexibles with his father in the 1970s—combining his father's excellent sales experience with Irv's vision to build a company and culture that would foster joy and innovation. Irv led the business for decades, and today remains a consultant to the business, helping with the transition to new owners and providing support on product development and new product launches.

Within Robbie and beyond, Irv describes himself as a "relationship enhancer"—serving as a mentor and making connections to build capacity within and between people. He brings these skills and interests to his work supporting local non-profits through leadership and philanthropy. In addition, Irv is passionate about learning and seeking fun and adventure, with growing opportunities in this domains since his transition from day-to-day leadership.

Irv's Tips for Successful Transition

- Start early. Have a good team in place that has been tested with the ability to take on larger roles. Communicate with other family members early and often. If possible, experiment with some outside activities beyond the business to learn what you may enjoy before you make the transition.
- Think about the things that you really enjoyed in the business, things you were good at, and where you could apply those things beyond the family business.
- Consider what makes your heart sing, what you want your purpose in life to be. Actually develop your purpose as early in life as you can. A long

time ago, I defined mine as "Make a positive difference in the lives of others." When I am fulfilling my purpose my heart sings, and there is joy. I now have more time to do that in different ways than before.

Frank Schurz, Schurz Communication

About the Company

- Schurz Communications was founded in 1872 by Alfred B. Miller and Elmer Crockett, who created the *South Bend Tribune*, the first Schurz newspaper.
- The company is a news and information business based in Mishawaka, Indiana, comprising newspaper publishing, phone directories, cable, and digital media.
- The company publishes multiple daily and weekly newspapers in medium and small markets. It previously also had a number of radio and television stations.
- Schurz became a broadcasting pioneer in 1922 when it launched WGAZ Radio (now WSBT) in South Bend, Indiana.

About the Interviewee

Frank Schurz is a fourth-generation family member who became president of Schurz Communication in 1982, and served in this capacity through 2007. In addition, Frank served on the board, including as chairman, through 2016. During his tenure, Schurz Communications Inc. (SCI) became a multimedia holding company in traditional media. The family's roots are in newspaper publishing, where it retains a significant position in many US markets.

Frank plays no role in the business today, other than serving as a mentor to nephews involved in the business, and attending family shareholder gatherings—though he has given his shares to his nieces and nephews. Today, Frank's focus is primarily on philanthropy and service on non-profit boards, with a strong interest in education and conservation.

Frank's Tips for Successful Transition

- Have interests and activities that have been cultivated well in advance of retirement.
- Take a hobby and turn it into a passion and then into an obsession.

Appendix 2: Interview Questions

Thank you for agreeing to speak with me about your transition out of leadership and into the future you have built for yourself. Very little has been written on how CEOs and other key driven business leaders continue to contribute once they have exited their business leadership role. It is my hope that sharing models of success—from other successful CEOs—will provide insight and hope, and serve to facilitate generational transitions for others going forward.

1) Tell me about your tenure as CEO/leader of your family's business…

    - What were main responsibilities? Board role (if any)?
    - What did you most enjoy in these roles?
    - How long did you serve in that capacity?

2) While you were the CEO did you have any other significant "life pursuits" or priorities that consumed meaningful time and energy from you? (e.g., active role in your church, significant volunteering, competitive athlete…)

    - If so, what were they and how much time did you devote to these?
    - How did these fit in with your day job?
    - What did you get out of these activities?

3) What led you to start planning for a transition away from the CEO role?

    - Triggering event (self/family/business/other) and what you remember feeling about the idea of transition, in general, at the time?
    - Do you remember any specific worries or concerns that you had at that time?

- To whom did you turn for advice, counsel, and support as you began to think about this significant life change?

4) From my research and experience with family business CEOs, this transition impacts the individual, their family, and their business—tell me about the steps you had to take to prepare yourself, your family, and your business:

   - Was there anything in place, a model or example you could look to for guidance?
   - What could have been done better or differently with hindsight?
   - Which do you think was the hardest to prepare?

5) How has this transition impacted your personal relationships?

   - Spouse, kids, business colleagues, other friends…
   - What surprised you in these changes?

6) Tell me about the journey or time between your "retiring" and arriving at the life you have today?

   - How long did it take?
   - Did you have clarity on what you wanted to do from the outset—or has there been an evolution and, if so, what has that been like? What do you think helped you understand the right steps/destination?
   - Did you have the right "network" to help you develop and access meaningful opportunities for this next phase of your life? If not, what did you do to broaden your network as needed?
   - How do your current pursuits impact others (spouse, kids, friends, community) and in what way did that drive or influence the direction you took for this phase of life?

7) How would you describe your role(s) or what you do today?

   - Did you encounter any resistance in establishing a new role for yourself? How did you work through that?
   - Did you have to demonstrate your value or otherwise carve out a role?

8) Tell me about your life today—what occupies your time?

   - Where do you feel you add the most value?
   - Where is your passion—how does your passion for this work compare to the passion you had for leading your family's business in the past?

- What are you most proud of in your current occupations? What fulfillment do you gain from them?
- How do you allocate/balance your time between CORE ACTIVITY, family, family business, philanthropy, leisure, other… What, if anything, is the other?

9) Today, in what way (if any) do you maintain a connection to the enterprise without overstepping your authority or otherwise "getting in the way"?

- What role(s) (formal or informal) do you have with the enterprise today?
- How much time do you devote to the family enterprise?
- How does connection to your family's business help you in your current primary pursuits?

10) What advice would you offer to other CEOs about how to plan for this?

- What are some unexpected pitfalls or struggles you encountered we haven't yet discussed?
- What are some joys and triumphs you wouldn't have expected?
- Is there a particularly important "key" to your success to which you would point?

11) Is there anything I haven't asked that you think it is important that we know or understand?

Appendix 3: Scoring Guides for Assessment Tools

Chapter 3

Table 3.1: Centrality of Work Role

Please circle the answer to the right of each question that most closely reflects your response.

QUESTION	Score to attribute for each answer below:				
	1	2	3	4	5
For how many years have you been in your current role?	Less than 5 years	5 to 10 years	10 to 15 years	15 to 20 years	Over 20 years
How many hours a week do you work on average?	20 or less	20 to 40	40 to 55	56 to 70	Over 70
How hard would it be to come up with something to do if you were suddenly presented with a day free from any work responsibilities?	Very Easy	Easy	I'd figure something out	Hard	Very Hard
How often does your work or company come up in conversations when you are not at work?	Almost never	Rarely	About half the time	Pretty regularly	Always
You check and respond to phone call, email or texts from work in the evenings, on weekends & on vacation	Almost never	Rarely	About half the time	Pretty regularly	Always
How many substantive interests do you have outside of work to which you regularly commit time and energy?	More than 5	3 to 5	1 to 2	1	0
How many <u>good friends</u> do you have that have nothing to do with your work life?	More than 5	3 to 5	1 to 2	1	0
If you had to introduce yourself without referencing your work, how hard would it be to come up with a description of who you are?	Very Easy	Easy	I'd figure something out	Hard	Very Hard
TALLY YOUR SCORE (number of responses per column times the allocated score)	_x 1	_x 2	_x 3	_x 4	_x 5
FINAL SCORE = SUM: _____	=____ +	____ +	____ +	____ +	____

Appendix 3: Scoring Guides for Assessment Tools

Scoring Guide 3.1: Centrality of Work Role

Understanding your Score:

- Between 8 – 20: You likely have clear boundaries to your work role
- Between 20 – 30: Suggests your work role is a dominant one for you
- Above 30: The centrality of your work role may make it harder for you to develop other aspects of your life

Table 3.2: Role Allocation

Please use the first column to allocate how you spend your time today, the second column to allocate how you would LIKE to be spending your time, and the third to note some obstacles you anticipate in moving towards that desired state.

ROLE	Percentage of your waking time (today)	Percentage of your waking time (desired allocation)	Obstacles in moving towards that desired state
Primary Work Role (Job)			
Other Business or Professional Roles (Board, mentor, side ventures, trade assoc., etc.)			
Spouse			
Other Family Relationships (time with children, extended family…)			
Friends			
Engaging with Faith or Spirituality			
Volunteer			
Pursuing meaningful hobby, fitness, or sport			
Other:			
Other:			
TOTAL	100%	100%	

Chapter 4

Table 4.1: General Readiness for Change*

Circle the number beside each statement that reflects how accurately the statement describes you in general. Please don't overthink your responses – go with your clearest impression.

Not Like Me	A little like me	A lot like me	Exactly Like Me
1	2	3	4

1. I prefer the familiar to the unknown　　　　　　　　　　1　2　3　4
2. I get impatient when there are no clear answers　　　　　1　2　3　4
3. I am inclined to establish routines and stay with them　　1　2　3　4
4. When something important doesn't work out, it takes me time to adjust　　1　2　3　4
5. I get frustrated when I can't get a grip on something　　 1　2　3　4
6. I prefer staying with the tried and true approach to things　1　2　3　4
7. I find it hard to give up on something, even if it isn't working out　1　2　3　4
8. I can't stand to leave things unfinished　　　　　　　　　1　2　3　4

SCORING Add up all the numbers you circled, for a TOTAL: _____

*Questionnaire adapted from instrument used by Professor T.J. Jenney, Purdue University, www.tech.purdue.edu/ols/courses/ols386/crispo/changereadinesstest.doc (accessed April 19, 2017)

Scoring Guide 4.1: General Readiness for Change

Understanding your Score:

- Between 8 – 16: You likely are quite comfortable with change
- Between 17 – 24: You may sometimes struggle with change
- Above 25: Suggests change is particularly difficult for you in most cases

Table 4.2: Openness to Experience*

Please review the statements below and answer honestly how regularly these statements are 'true for you' using the following numbers to score your responses:

Disagree Strongly	Disagree a litte	Neither agree nor disagree	Agree a little	Agree strongly
1	2	3	4	5

1. ____ Tends more towards imaginative rather than pragmatic approaches
2. ____ Is curious to learn about many different things
3. ____ Is less drawn to traditional ideas than to creative ones
4. ____ Is quick to understand new ideas or approaches
5. ____ Is sophisticated in art, music, or literature
6. ____ Is interested in abstract ideas
7. ____ Is drawn to 'out of the box' thinking
8. ____ Is creative or inventive
9. ____ Is less traditional in my interests than most
10. ____ Has good non-traditional ideas

_____: SUM up your scores for all 10 statements for a TOTAL SCORE

*Adapted from scales described by Hao Zhao and Scott E. Seibert in "The Big Five Personality Dimensions and Entrepreneurial Status: A Meta-Analytic Review," *Journal of Applied Psychology*, 91(2), pp. 259–271.

Scoring Guide 4.2: Openness to Experience

Understanding your Score:

- The range of possible scores is from 10 – 50, with a higher number indicating a greater 'openness to new experiences.'

Table 4.3: Desire for Control*

Please review the statements below and answer honestly how regularly these statements are 'true for you' using the following numbers to score your responses:

Never	Seldom	Sometimes	Frequently	Always
1	2	3	4	5

1. ____ I enjoy being able to influence the actions of others.
2. ____ I enjoy having control over my own destiny.
3. ____ My ideas are good and I try to persuade other people to accept them.
4. ____ I only share information with others when I feel they are ready to hear it.
5. ____ I try to avoid situations where someone else tries to tell me what to do.
6. ____ I like to be in charge of things.
7. ____ I am concerned about my reputation.
8. ____ I try to do better than other people on things that I do.

_____: SUM up your scores for all 8 statements for a TOTAL SCORE

*Scale adapted from Desirability of Control Scale published in Jerry Burger, *Desire for Control: Personality, Social & Clinical Perspectives*, Plenum Press, 1992.

Scoring Guide 4.3: Desire for Control

Understanding your Score:

- Below 18: Reflects a lower need to be in charge or in control than most business leaders
- Between 19 – 31: Reflects a moderate need to be in charge or in control
- Above 32: Suggests a relatively strong need to be in charge or in control

Table 4.4: Servant Leadership Style

In thinking about how you typically approach your work responsibilities, please indicate your level of agreement or disagreement with the following statements. Please answer the questions as honestly as possible – considering how others might perceive you as a 'gut check'.

Disagree strongly	Disagree a litte	Agree a little	Agree strongly
1	2	3	4

I support others in their efforts to do their best work	1	2	3	4
Good bosses make all employees feel important	1	2	3	4
I try to communicate a welcoming attitude to everyone I meet	1	2	3	4
I constantly look for ways to serve others	1	2	3	4
I almost always see the positive potential in others	1	2	3	4
I work hard to try to enrich the lives of those who are less fortunate than me	1	2	3	4
I work to create an environment where each person feels understood	1	2	3	4
My first priority in life is to serve	1	2	3	4
I encourage others to provide me with constructive criticism of my performance so I can improve	1	2	3	4
I get immense pleasure from seeing others grow & develop	1	2	3	4

Add up all the numbers you circled to tally a TOTAL SCORE: _____

Scoring 4.4: Servant Leadership Style

Understanding your Score:

- Below 20: Reflects a more directive leadership style
- Between 21 – 30: Refl ects a moderate tendency towards servant leadership
- Above 31: Suggests a strong tendency towards servant leadership style

 Table 4.5: Capacity for Disengagement and Reengagement*

During their lives people cannot always attain what they want and are sometimes forced to stop pursuing the goals they have set. How do you usually react when this happens to you?

Please indicate the extent to which you agree or disagree with each of the following statements, as it usually applies to you.

Disagree Strongly	Disagree a litte	Neither agree nor disagree	Agree a little	Agree strongly
1	2	3	4	5

If I have to stop pursuing an important goal in my life:

I stay committed to the goal for a long time; I can't let it go	1	2	3	4	5
It's difficult for me to stop thinking about the goal	1	2	3	4	5
I find it difficult to reduce my desire to achieve the goal	1	2	3	4	5
It's hard for me to reduce my effort towards the goal	1	2	3	4	5

SUM up above scores for a total on **Disengagement:** _____

I seek other meaningful goals	1	2	3	4	5
I convince myself that I have other meaningful goals to pursue	1	2	3	4	5
I start working on other new goals	1	2	3	4	5
I think about other new goals to pursue	1	2	3	4	5
I tell myself that I have a number of other new goals to draw upon	1	2	3	4	5
I put effort toward other meaningful goals	1	2	3	4	5

SUM up above scores for a total on **Reengagement:** _____

*Questionnaire Adapted from Goal Adjustment Capacity Scale in C. Wrosch, M. Scheier, G. Miller, R. Schulz, and C. Carver, "Adaptive self-regulation of unattainable goals: Goal disengagement, goal reengagement, and subjective well-being," *Personality and Social Psychology Bulletin*, 2003, 29, pp. 1491–1508.

Scoring Guide 4.5: Capacity for Disengagement and Reengagement

Understanding your Disengagement Score:

- Below 8: Suggests you have a relatively easy time letting go of goals
- Between 9 – 12: Reflects some challenges for you to let go of goals
- Above 13: Suggests abandoning important goals is particularly difficult for you

Understanding your Reengagement Score:

- 25 or greater: Suggests you have a good deal of ease finding & committing to new goals
- Between 13 – 24: Suggests you are sometimes challenged to engage in new goals
- Below 13: Indicates you may really struggle to find and commit to new goals

Chapter 5

 Table 5.4: Assessing Family Stakeholder Readiness

Please use the below to assess the extent to which you believe various stakeholders feel 'ready' for your eventual transition out of the leadership role.

STAKEHOLDER GROUPS	GENERAL LEVEL of 'READINESS' or COMFORT with TRANSITION	VIEW OF BUSINESS GOING FORWARD…	IMPACT of TRANSITION on PERSONAL RELATIONSHIP	IDEAS ON ADDRESSING CONCERNS
CURRENT GENERATION				
Your spouse	High (calm) Uncertain Low (worried)	Good Unsure Worried	Will improve Unsure Will strain	
Sibling Shareholders (if any)	High (calm) Uncertain Low (worried)	Good Unsure Worried	Will improve Unsure Will strain	
Other (fill in)	High (calm) Uncertain Low (worried)	Good Unsure Worried	Will improve Unsure Will strain	
NEXT GENERATION				
Your children working in business (if any)	High (calm) Uncertain Low (worried)	Good Unsure Worried	Will improve Unsure Will strain	
Your children not working in business (if any)	High (calm) Uncertain Low (worried)	Good Unsure Worried	Will improve Unsure Will strain	
Other family working in business (if any)	High (calm) Uncertain Low (worried)	Good Unsure Worried	Will improve Unsure Will strain	
Other family shareholders	High (calm) Uncertain Low (worried)	Good Unsure Worried	Will improve Unsure Will strain	
Other (fill in)	High (calm) Uncertain Low (worried)	Good Unsure Worried	Will improve Unsure Will strain	

Chapter 6

Table 6.1: How Ready is Your Business for Transition?

Please assess your business' level of 'readiness' on the seven dimensions below.

Evaluate your business along each of these dimensions:	Score to attribute for each answer below:				
	5	4	3	2	1
Ownership Group Alignment	Very Ready	Mostly Ready	Marginally Ready	Some Steps Taken	No Progress
Company's Position in Industry	Dominant	Strong	Good	Marginal	Weak
Financial Condition of Business	Very Strong	Strong	Modest	Marginal	Weak
Successor Capability	Excellent	Very Strong	Good	Marginal	Weak
Next Generation Management Team	Excellent	Very Strong	Good	Marginal	Weak
Professional Board of Directors	Excellent & longstanding	Very good	Getting established	Informal	Weak
Written Strategic Plan	Strong & widely supported	Solid	Being developed	Rough ideas	We don't plan
SUM of POINTS: _____					

Scoring Guide 6.1: How Ready is Your Business for Transition?

Understanding your Score:

- Below 15: Suggests some weakness in the business may complicate transition process
- Between 16 – 24: The business could be strengthened further to help facilitate transition
- Above 25: Suggests the business is in a strong position to navigate transition

Table 6.2: Confidence in Prospective Successor

Please review the statements below, and indicate to what degree you believe they are strengths of the prospective successor for leadership in your business:

Not at all	A little	Somewhat	A great deal	A lot
1	2	3	4	5

Making good business decisions	1 ☐	2 ☐	3 ☐	4 ☐	5 ☐
Developing a strong and empowered senior leadership team	1 ☐	2 ☐	3 ☐	4 ☐	5 ☐
Having the right experience and judgment to bring to challenging situations	1 ☐	2 ☐	3 ☐	4 ☐	5 ☐
Nurturing the culture and reputation of the business	1 ☐	2 ☐	3 ☐	4 ☐	5 ☐
Managing the company's financial health in line with strategic goals	1 ☐	2 ☐	3 ☐	4 ☐	5 ☐
Developing strong & trusting bonds with other owners	1 ☐	2 ☐	3 ☐	4 ☐	5 ☐
Effectively using the board and other key advisors	1 ☐	2 ☐	3 ☐	4 ☐	5 ☐
Growing the company					
SUM of POINTS: _____					

Scoring Guide 6.2: Confidence in Prospective Successor

Understanding your Score:

- Above 35: Suggests you have tremendous confidence in successor's ability to thrive
- Between 20 – 34: Suggests you believe there are still some gaps in your successor's development
- Below 20: Implies a level of concern around your successor's abilities and readiness that is likely to get in the way of a successful transition process

Appendix 3: Scoring Guides for Assessment Tools

Chapter 8

Table 8.1: Importance of Impact

Please indicate, on a scale of 1 to 4 the extent to which you agree with the following statements…

Not at all	A little	Somewhat	A lot
1	2	3	4

Statement	1	2	3	4
I want to be at the forefront of new ideas or involved with substantive innovation…	1☐	2☐	3☐	4☐
I want my actions or decisions to change a lot of lives…	1☐	2☐	3☐	4☐
It is important to me that my ideas influence others…	1☐	2☐	3☐	4☐
I want to leave a legacy	1☐	2☐	3☐	4☐
It is important to me that my ideas are adopted	1☐	2☐	3☐	4☐
It is important to me that I can see the results of my efforts…	1☐	2☐	3☐	4☐
It is important to me that my life will have made a big difference to others…	1☐	2☐	3☐	4☐
SUM of POINTS: _____				

Scoring Guide 8.1: Importance of Impact

Understanding your Score:

- A score of 21 or higher: Suggests making an impact is of greater importance to you than it might be to others
- A score below 12: Might suggest direct impact is not as a high a priority to you as it could be to others

Table 8.2: Individual Drivers*

When it comes to any activity we may pursue, we are all motivated by different things. Please rank the following common motivators (or "drivers") in terms of importance to you by distributing a total of 100 points among those items that are your most important motivators.

The item that is the greatest motivator to you will have the most points associated with it. For example, if you are mostly driven to help others, then "Altruism" would receive more points than any other item. Please spread your 100 points among a minimum of three drivers.

It's okay to have some drivers with 0 points (which would mean that those items do not matter to you at all). Try to be as honest with yourself as possible – there are no 'better' drivers than others. Get input from people who know you well if you feel their insights will help.

Driver	Description	Points (Total to 100)
Recognition	Appreciate attention, visibility, approval, and praise	
Control	Desire for success, accomplishment, status, and control	
Fun	Orientation for fun, pleasure, and enjoyment	
Altruism	Desire to help others and contribute to society	
Affiliation	Desire for and enjoyment of social interaction and strong people connections	
Tradition	Dedication, strong personal beliefs, attachment to culture and norms	
Security	Need for predictability, structure, and order	
Commerce	Interest in money, profits, investment, and business opportunities	
Aesthetics	Need for self-expression, concern over look, feel, and design	
Science	Quest for knowledge, research, technology, and data	
	Total	100

*Exercise adapted from Hogan, R., & Hogan, J. (2007). Hogan Personality Inventory manual (3rd ed.). Tulsa, OK: Hogan Assessment Systems.

Chapter 9

 **Table 9.3: Overall Readiness Assessment**

Using a scale of 1 to 5, Please use the first column to 'score' the level of readiness you perceive in each of the core dimensions of the model that has been discussed in this book. Use the same scale to indicate how hard you think it will be to make any needed changes in that dimension and use the third column to note some ideas for progress.

DIMENSION	READINESS SCORE Scale of 1 to 5 1 = There is a lot of change needed here, to 5 = Excellent, feels 'ready'	EASE TO ADDRESS Scale of 1 to 5 1 = Will be very hard to change, to 5 = Can and already is changing	IDEAS FOR HOW TO MOVE FORWARD
INTERNAL			
Identity: Job no longer as central to your sense of 'self'			
Temperament: Open to new experiences & need for control			
Change Capacity: Ease in letting go of goals & developing new ones			
FAMILY			
Relationships: Strong marriage and family bonds			
Healthy/effective communication			
BUSINESS			
Ownership alignment			
Financial/market strength of enterprise			
Successor team strength			
Strength/depth of governance systems			

Recommended Readings and Other Resources

Books

Aronoff and Ward, *Family Business Ownership* (Palgrave Macmillan, New York, 2011).
William Bridges, *Transitions: Making Sense of Life's Changes* (Da Capo Press, Cambridge, 2004).
William Bridges and Susan Bridges, *Managing Transitions* (Da Capo Press, Cambridge, 2009).
Bob Buford, *Half Time: Moving from Success to Significance* (Zondervan, Grand Rapids Michigan, 2008).
Peter Buffett, *Life Is What You Make It* (Harmony Books, New York, 2010).
Randel Carlock and John L. Ward, *When Family Businesses Are Best: The Parallel Planning Process for Family Harmony and Business Success* (Palgrave Macmillan, New York, 2010).
David Corbett, *Portfolio Life* (Jossey-Bass, San Francisco, 2012).
Stephen Covey, *The Seven Habits of Highly Effective People: Powerful Lessons in Personal Change* (Simon & Schuster, New York, 1989).
Mihaly Csikszentmihalyi, *Flow: The Psychology of Optimal Experience* (Harper Perennial, New York, 2008).
Chris Eckrich and Steve McClure, *The Family Council Handbook* (Palgrave Macmillan, New York, 2012).
Erik Erikson, *The Life Cycle Completed*, 9th ed. (Norton, New York, 1997).
Marc Freedman, *The Big Shift: Navigating the New Stage Beyond Midlife* (Hachette, New York, 2012).
Betty Friedan, *Fountain of Age* (Simon & Schuster, New York, 1993).
Robert Hill, Seven Strategies for Positive Aging (W.W. Norton & Co., New York, 2008).

James Hunter, *The Servant* (Crown Business, New York, 2008).

Robert Kegan and Lisa Laskow Lahey, *Resistance to Change: How to Overcome It and Unlock the Potential in Yourself and Your Organization* (Harvard Business Press, Cambridge, 2009).

Kelly Lecouvie and Jennifer Pendergast, *Family Business Succession: Your Roadmap to Continuity* (Palgrave Macmillan, New York, 2014).

Daniel Levinson, *The Seasons of a Man's Life* (Random House Publishing House, New York, 1978).

Pendergast, Ward & Brun de Pontet, *Building a Successful Family Business Board* (Palgrave Macmillan, New York, 2011).

Michael Porter, *Competitive Strategy: Techniques for Analyzing Industries and Competitors* (Free Press, New York, 1998).

Ransberg, Sage-Howard, and Schuman, *Human Resources in the Family Business* (Palgrave Macmillan, New York, 2016).

Nancy Schlossberg, *Revitalizing Retirement: Reshaping your Identity, Relationships, and Purpose* (American Psychological Association, Washington, DC, 2009).

George Vaillant, *Aging Well* (Little, Brown and Co., Boston, 2002).

Andrew Weil, *Healthy Aging: A Lifelong Guide to Your Well-Being* (Anchor Books, New York, 2005).

Articles and Speeches

David Brooks TED talk (March, 2014) Should you live for your resume… or your eulogy? https://www.ted.com/talks/david_brooks_should_you_live_for_your_resume_or_your_eulogy (TED Talk).

Neal Gabler, The Secret Shame of Middle Class Americans, *The Atlantic*, May 2016. http://www.theatlantic.com/magazine/archive/2016/05/my-secret-shame/476415/

Barton Goldsmith, 7 Questions That Can Strengthen Your Relationship, *Psychology Today*, August 6, 2014. https://www.psychologytoday.com/blog/emotional-fitness/201408/7-questions-can-strengthen-your-relationship (accessed April 25, 2017).

Daniel Goleman, Are Women More Emotionally Intelligent Than Men? *Psychology Today*, April 29, 2011. https://www.psychologytoday.com/blog/the-brain-and-emotional-intelligence/201104/are-women-more-emotionally-intelligent-men

Ivan Lansberg, The Tests of a Prince, *Harvard Business Review*, September 2007. https://hbr.org/2007/09/the-tests-of-a-prince

John D. Mayer, What Emotional Intelligence Is and Is Not, *Psychology Today*, September 21, 2009. https://www.psychologytoday.com/blog/the-personality-analyst/200909/what-emotional-intelligence-is-and-is-not

Stephen Miller, Developing Next Generation Leaders in a Family Business, Published by the Family Business Consulting Group. http://www.thefbcg.com/assets/1/22/FBA_Developing_Next_Generation_Leaders_SPM.pdf

Patricia Reaney, Ageism in U.S. Workforce: A Persistent Problem Unlikely to Go Away, *Reuters*, October 19, 2015. http://www.reuters.com/article/us-employment-discrimination-age-idUSKCN0SD1Z720151019

Carl Richards, Learning to Deal with the Imposter Syndrome, *New York Times*, October 26, 2015. https://www.nytimes.com/2015/10/26/your-money/learning-to-deal-with-the-impostor-syndrome.html

Lydia Saad, The "40-Hour" Work Week Is Actually Longer—by 7 Hours, *Gallup.com*, August 29, 2014. http://www.gallup.com/poll/175286/hour-workweek-actually-longer-seven-hours.aspx

Eli Watkins and Jami Gangel, George W. Bush Discovers His 'Inner Rembrandt' in Homage to Veterans, *CNN.com*, February 27, 2017. http://www.cnn.com/2017/02/27/politics/george-w-bush-paintings/

Other Resources and Organizations

American Association of Retired Persons (AARP). http://www.aarp.org/: A non-profit, non-partisan organization that helps people 50 and older improve the quality of their lives. As the energy and expectations of today's retired population has expanded, so have the range of services and opportunities that may be found under this broad umbrella.

Executive Service Corps (ESC). https://www.execservicecorps.org/: The mission of the Executive Service Corps is to make non-profits successful. They provide consulting, coaching, and professional services to other non-profit organizations and are always eager to find capable volunteer advisors.

National Association of Corporate Directors (NACD). https://www.nacdonline.org/: An independent, not-for-profit organization dedicated to advancing boardroom leadership. They provide classes in board governance. A certification from NACD may help your chances of being selected to serve on a board.

Service Corps of Retired Executives (SCORE). https://www.score.org/: A non-profit association dedicated to helping small businesses get off the ground, grow, and achieve their goals through education and mentorship. Retired executives are paired with local entrepreneurs to provide guidance and support through the auspices of the US Small Business Administration.

Notes

1. Some information from www.nixonmedical.com.
2. Some information from www.carlson.com.
3. Some information from www.clemensfamilycorp.com.
4. Some information from www.amway.com.
5. Some information from www.bushbeans.com.
6. Some information from www.joynadvisors.com.

Index[1]

A
Achievement-driven individuals, 45
Administrative support, 27, 28
Ageism, 21n1, 55, 56
Airbnb, 40
Allyn, E., 10, 23, 65, 115, 155, 156
American social norms, 101
Amway, 74, 161
Arts activity, 121–122
Athleticism, 25, 102

B
Babysitter, 68–69
Baillargeon, P., 155–157, 159, 160
Baillie, J., 38n5
Baum, A., 60n14
Benefits and status, loss of, 27–29
Benyamini, Y., 38n11
Berstein, M., 10, 119, 156
"Big Five" personality traits, 43
Brain games, 124
Bridges, S., 12n4

Bridges, W., 12n4, 38n1, 53, 136
Brooks, D., 150, 154n1
Brun de Pontet, S., 12n3, 60n16, 98n7
Buffet, P., 38n12, 59n5, 127
Buffett, W., 127
Burke, P. J., 38n4
Bush, G. W., 122
Bush Brothers & Company, 162
Business commitment, 94
Business leader, vi, 7, 15, 18–20, 32, 40, 44, 49, 63, 75–77, 106, 107, 113, 115, 146, 149, 150
  See also family business leader
Business leadership, 15, 18, 19, 41, 77, 106, 109, 122
  engagement in, 117
Business owners, advisors to, 8
Business readiness, 81–82
  assessment of, 96
  capable and trusted successor and, 92–95
  enterprise readiness and, 82–92
Business system, 63, 84, 92, 96, 143

---

[1] Note: Page numbers followed by "n" refer to notes

C

Cakebread, J., 11, 155, 156
Cakebread Cellars, 155
Canada, 101
Carlock, R., 12n1
Carlson, 69, 89, 104, 156
Carmelli, D., 59n11
Carter, J., 35
Carter Center, 35
Carver, C., 60n15, 60n17, 60n19
Castonguay, A., 60n21
CEO, vi, vii, 2–5, 8–10, 17–19, 21, 22, 26–29, 31, 34, 37, 39, 44–46, 50, 51, 53, 55–57, 61, 63–65, 67, 72, 77, 81, 85, 86, 89, 91, 93, 95, 105, 107, 112, 116, 118, 119, 122, 132, 138, 139, 149, 153, 167, 168
  family business, 26
  position of, 19, 24
  sacrifice of, 163–164
CFO position, 89, 90
Change, readiness for, 39–58
  aging indignities and, 53–56
  goal flexibility and, 49–52
  need for control and, 44–48
  openness to experience and, 43–44
  temperament and, 42–48
Cheerleader, 113, 157, 158
Children and grandchildren, connection with, 67–74
Circumstantial tests, 93
Civic engagement, 19, 102, 104, 122
Civic opportunity, 122
Clemens Family Corporation, 39, 89, 112, 120, 157
Clemens, P., 5, 11, 39, 45, 89, 112, 120, 157, 158
Cleveland Clinic board, 21
Cleveland Clinic hospital, 105
Closeness, divergent needs for, 72–73
Cohen, S., 60n14
Combat ageism, 110
Command-and-control leader, 49
Committed ownership, 83–84
Communication, promotion of, 75
Community leadership, 120, 122, 125
Community service, 20, 102
Conceptual model, 13–22
Conflicting interests, potential, 63
Continuity plans, for business, 138
Control, need for, 44–48
Corbett, D., 132n2
Costa, P., 59n4
Crane, L., 11, 36, 59, 158, 159
Crane & Company, 37, 59, 158
Creative destruction, 40
Csikszentmihalyi, M., 133n7
Cultural activities, 121–122
Cultural context, 21, 101
Cultural elements, 101–102

D

Dame, A., 59n11
Davos, 105
Day-to-day leadership, 10, 51, 69, 75, 99
Decision-making, 20, 21, 54, 55, 91
  authority, 28
Dent-making principle, 115
DeVos, D., 1, 5, 11, 74, 159, 160
Diverse board, 88
Driven leaders, 139

E

Eckrich, C., 80n5
Effective plan, 138
Emotional intelligence, 94, 98n6, 107
Enterprise readiness, 82–92
Erikson, E., 59n10, 59n12
Ethier, J., 2, 11, 77, 160, 161
Executive leadership, 18, 85
Extroversion, 42

F

Family bonding, 17, 73
Family business, viii, 8, 44, 64, 70, 74, 76, 93, 141, 155, 156, 160, 161, 163–165
Family business leader, 24, 39, 122
See also business leader
Family business leadership, 26, 50, 76, 144, 156
Family business systems, 1–4, 6, 8, 10, 15, 21, 23, 24, 144
  research of, 4–5
Family commitment, 94–95
Family council, 75, 76, 153
Family employees, feared loss of connection with, 69–71
Family enterprise leaders, sacrifice of, 161
Family leadership, *see* family business leadership
Family members, 2, 8, 17, 18, 21, 31, 46, 56, 57, 61, 67–72, 74–76, 92, 94, 162, 165
Family-owned enterprises, 162
Family readiness, 61–78, 178
  assessment of, 76–78
Family relationships, 18
Family stakeholders, 17, 75–77, 178
Family systems, 18, 56, 61, 63, 73, 76, 79, 81, 136, 143
Financial security, 81, 86
Financial stability, 81, 85–87
Fitness, 102, 124
Ford, H., 51
Fountain of Age (Friedan), 30, 38n10
France, 101
Freedman, M., 6, 12n8, 12n9, 60n22
Friedan, B., 30, 38n10
Fun activities, 124

G

Gabler, N., 98n2
Gallup, 24
Gangel, J., 132n3
Gee, S., 38n5
Geller, D., 11, 161
Goal flexibility, 49–53
Goleman, D., 107, 112n1
Good governance system, 73–76
GRPL box, 83

H

Hard-charging CEOs, 140
Hard-driving CEOs, 150
Health crisis, 53–54
Herschend Entertainment, 113
Herschend Family Entertainment, 162
Herschend, J., 11, 113, 132, 162
Hill, R., 60n18
Humans, as purpose driven, 6
Hunter, J., 98n8

I

IDEAL Industries, 163
Ideal successor, 92–95
Identity trap, 24, 25, 39, 102, 115
  avoidance of, 31–36
Incoming leader, 2, 18, 81, 82, 84, 88, 89, 91, 92, 94, 95
Intentional transition-related planning, 138
See also family readiness
Introversion, 42
Intrusion, unwanted, 64–67

J

Jenney, T. J., 59n3
Jobs, S., 115, 158, 159
Johns, G., 59n6
JOYN, 161
Juday, D., 11, 31, 81, 163

K

Kahneman, D., 59n9
Kegan, R., 59n1
Kets de Vries, Manfred F.R., 12n5

L

Lahey, L. L., 59n1
Lansberg, I., 93, 98n5
Leadership, 2, 15, 63, 71, 119–124
  See also specific entries
Leadership transitions, 13
Lecouvie, K., 12n2, 147n2
Levinson, H., 12n11
Life partner, 62–67
Life transitions, 61
Local community, 103, 109, 119, 122
Lomranz, J., 38n11

M

Mandatory retirement age, 89, 140
Marital partner, 62–67
Martire, L., 60n14
Matthews, K., 60n14
Mayer, J. D., 98n6
McClure, S., 80n5
McCrae, R., 59n4
Mentorship, 58, 95, 130–132
Miller, G., 60n17, 60n19
Miller, S., 98n4
Musée de l'Homme, 158

N

Nelson, M. C., 11, 34, 69, 89, 104, 156, 157
Network, people in, 105–108
Neutral zone, 136
Next-generation leaders, 84, 90
Next-generation owners, 84
Nisen, M., 38n7
Nixon Uniform Service and Medical Wear, 119, 156

Non-family CEO, 75
Non-family leader, 88
Non-profit boards, 120, 165
Non-profit leadership, 119–122
Non-work-related commitments, 5
North American culture, 22, 23
Nuclear family, 61, 67

O

Openness, to experience, 43
Outgoing leader, 2, 4, 81, 84, 85, 88, 89, 92, 94, 95, 105
Outside-of-work organization, 58

P

Paradox-related skills, 142
Parent–adult child relationship, 67
Passions, identifying, 128–129
Pendergast, J., 12n2, 147n2
Pennsylvania-based Clemens Family Corporation, 3
Perks, access to, 28, 35
Personal continuity, viii, 3, 4, 7, 9, 15, 62, 159, 162, 163, 165, 167
Planning, 7
  See also specific entries
Playful pursuits, 124
Personal continuity planning, 7, 113, 152
  See also specific entries
Personal Continuity Readiness model, 13, 15–17, 39
Personal readiness, 13–16, 18, 20, 24, 40, 82, 99, 113, 143
  improvement of, 56–58
Personality
  goal flexibility and, 49
  need for control and, 44
  openness to experience and, 43
  temperament and, 42–48
Personality style, 47
Personality traits, 46

Physical activity, 102
Picchu, M., 125
Political engagement, 102, 122
Political leadership, 122
Political opportunity, 122
Political tests, 93
Porter, M., 98n1
Post-career stage, 116
Post-CEO roles, 3
Post-CEO vocation, 166–167
Post-leadership, 5, 54, 128, 141
Post-retirement, 1, 67, 105
   decline, 107
   life, 107
Post-work life, 1, 4, 5, 8, 11, 15, 17, 23, 30, 37, 39, 47, 56, 58, 67, 99, 105, 111, 113, 117, 121, 130, 139
Post-work opportunities, 19, 54, 104, 118, 121
Post-work plan, 139
Professional development, 92
Professional identity, recognizing over-commitment to, 34
Professional leadership, 119–121, 126

Q

Qualifying tests, 93

R

Readiness assessment, 144
Reengagement, 4, 54, 57, 59n17, 177
   definition of, 51
   goal disengagement and, 49–52
Reitzes, D. C., 38n4
Relationships, loss of, 56–57
Retired CEO, 64, 65, 70, 72, 73, 77
   See also retirement
Retirement, 1, 4–7, 10, 15–18, 23–31, 33, 35, 39, 41, 43–45, 51–58, 108, 114–117, 119, 122, 124–126, 130, 131, 136, 138–140, 143, 144, 160, 163
   as challenging transition, 25
   See also specific entries
Retirement plans, 4, 58, 61, 116, 143
Retiring family business leaders, 105
   See also specific entries
Richards, C., 98n3
Roadblocks, 133–139
Robbie Fantastic Flexibles, 20, 67, 118, 147, 164
Robinson, I., 11, 20, 67, 118, 147, 164
Rock, R., 38n9
Rosenman, R., 59n11

S

Sabiston, C., 60n21
Saks, A., 59n6
Scheier, M., 60n14, 60n15, 60n17, 60n19
Schlossberg, N., 12n7, 12n10
Schlossberg, S., 38n6
Schulz, R., 60n14, 60n15, 60n17, 60n19
Schumpter, J., 40, 59n2
Schurz, F., 1, 11, 95, 109, 165
Schurz Communication, 1, 95, 165
Seibert, S. E., 59n7, 59n8
Self-imposed tests, 93
Senior generation, 160
Senior-generation leaders, 90
Serenity Prayer, 140
Servant leadership, 45–48, 95, 98n8, 176
The Seven Habits of Highly Effective People (Covey), 24
Shareholders, 18, 24, 74, 75, 85, 88, 92, 116, 153
SMART, *see* specific, measurable, achievable, realistic, and time (SMART)
Smith, J., 16
Social context, 20, 101

Social network, 105–107, 121
Social norms, 101, 109
Specific, measurable, achievable, realistic, and time (SMART) goals, 145, 146
Stakeholders, 2, 17, 63, 70, 74, 75, 77, 82, 84, 88–90, 92–94, 136, 140, 142, 149, 150, 154, 178
Steinem, G., 55, 60n22
Strategic planning process, 69, 87, 91, 92, 133, 147, 150
Successful retirement, 10
Succession planning, ii, 2, 3, 145n2
Sustainable structures and processes, 87–92
Sutter, J., 132n1
System readiness, 9, 16–21, 62, 82, 92, 100
Swan, G., 59n11

T

Temperament, 69, 107
  personality and, 42–48
Texas, 21
Transitioning business leaders, family members of, 8
Transitioning leader, 69, 120, 121, 135
  personal readiness for, 15–17
Transition process, 27, 32, 42, 47, 81, 87
Transitions (Bridges), 53

Tversky, A., 59n9
Type-A CEOs, 7
Type A people, *see* achievement-driven individuals

U

Uber, 40
United States, 101
US Baby Boomer population, 22n1

V

Vaillant, G., 12n6, 124
Volunteering, centrality of, 102

W

Ward, J. L., 12n1
Watkins, E., 132n3
Welch Allyn, 23, 65, 115, 153
Wofford, J., 12n11
Work-based relationships, 106
Work-based social network, 106
Work-related roles, 26
Wrosch, C., 60n14, 60n15, 60n17, 60n19, 60n21

Z

Zdaniuk, B., 60n14
Zhao, H., 59n7, 59n8

The manufacturer's authorised representative in the EU is Springer Nature Customer Service Centre GmbH, Europaplatz 3, 69115 Heidelberg, Germany. If you have any concerns regarding our products, please contact ProductSafety@springernature.com

Printed and bound by CPI Group (UK) Ltd, Croydon, CR0 4YY

25/03/2026

02078234-0001